PILLARS OF LEADERSHIP

PILLARS
OF LEADERSHIP

David J. Vaughan

Published by Cumberland House Publishing, Inc., 431 Harding Industrial Drive, Nashville, Tennessee 37211.

Cover design by Bruce Gore, Gore Studios, Inc.
Text design by Heather Armstrong

Library of Congress Cataloging-in-Publication Data

Vaughan, David J., 1955–
    The pillars of leadership / David J. Vaughan.
        p. cm.—(Leaders in action)
    Includes bibliographical references.
    ISBN 1-58182-060-7 (pbk. : alk. paper)
    1. Leadership. I. Title. II. Leaders in action series.
HM1261.V38   2000
303.3'4—dc21   00-021345

Printed in the United States of America
 2 3 4 5 6 7 8 — 04 03 02 01

To my wife, Diane Lynn Vaughan:

I know a thing that's most uncommon;
(Envy, be silent and attend!)
I know a reasonable woman,
Handsome and witty, yet a friend.
Not warp'd by passion, awed by rumour;
Not grave through pride, nor gay through folly;
An equal mixture of good-humour
And sensible soft melancholy.
"Has she no faults then (Envy says), Sir?"
Yes, she one, I must aver:
When all the world conspires to praise her,
The woman's deaf, and does not hear.

— Alexander Pope, 1688–1744

TABLE OF CONTENTS

FOREWORD

by George Grant

A t the Constitutional Convention in 1787, James Madison was one of the most active speakers—and many wise provisions in the final document owe their origin to his foresight and learning. Deeply versed in theories of governance and profoundly affected by his Christian faith, he realized only too well that his gravest flaw was a tendency to become rather over-zealous during debate.

Along with Alexander Hamilton and John Jay, Madison wrote the brilliant Federalist Papers and was the trusted advisor and confidante of both George Washington and Thomas Jefferson. Later, he would himself occupy the White House and make a unique mark upon the fledgling nation's highest office during particularly difficult days. But it was at the Convention that his gifts were most evident and his star shone brightest.

Knowing he was apt to get carried away when addressing the Convention, he asked a fellow delegate from Virginia to sit by his side and tweak his coattails if he seemed to be getting too obviously excited. Later that very day, after a particularly impassioned discourse, he sat down—hot, perspiring, and exhausted. Turning as with a sudden realization, he reproached his friend for not pulling at his coat, thus tempering his firebrand oratory.

"I would just as soon have laid a finger on the lightning," said the awestruck man.

Similar stories are told of many of the founding fathers. When Patrick Henry spoke his hearers were utterly mesmerized. When Samuel Adams addressed his fellow patriots, it was said that he spoke with the voice of the divine. And when Peyton Randolph rose, an admiring silence always seemed to envelope the hall.

There is a power in unswerving conviction that inevitably arrests the attentions of both men and nations. There is an almost indescribable appeal that attaches itself to uncompromising vision and principled passion. And this fact is illustrated, not just in the American founding era, as remarkable as it was, but throughout all of history. The stories David Vaughan has assembled in this book demonstrate this only too well.

Each of the men he profiles was a man of principle. Each was a man of conviction. Each was somehow able to catalyze situations and circumstances, against all odds, to advance the cause of beauty, goodness, and truth, which are but the essential constituent parts of Western Civilization. Each refused to be drawn into the petty world of peccant patronizing. Each was a wise man who simply would not sacrifice integrity for pragmatism, honor for profit, or principle for efficiency. They didn't wait for polling data to determine what was right and good and true. They did not hesitate in the face of fierce opposition or stern fashion.

In other words, they were leaders.

According to the great English pundit and critic, Samuel Johnson, a leader is "by passion, by conviction, and by unswerving determination, a man who bears in his life both the most tangible and intangible qualities of heart and mind and flesh." He wisely concludes, "Best we study these well."

But what is it exactly that makes a man a leader? What character traits are necessary to steer men and nations into the way they should go? What constitutes genuine leadership? Where does unswerving passion, undaunting conviction, and unflinching determination come from? How are we to "study well" that which is both "the most tangible and intangible" simultaneously?

Dr. Vaughan has raised these vital issues in *The Pillars of Leadership*. He regales us with many delightful stories. He entertains us with tales of valor, wisdom, and virtue. He introduces us to true characters whose lives are marked by the unmistakable signs of true character. But more importantly, he affords us with insights into the essence of this palpable power of conviction. In other words, he shows us not only what great leaders do, but what they are. As a result, this is one leadership book that defies the genre, breaking new ground.

And for that, we can all be grateful.

ACKNOWLEDGMENTS

*E*merson once commented "the only reward of virtue is virtue; the only way to have a friend is to be one." I can only hope that I have been a friend who is worthy of so many faithful friends and family members who have encouraged me in my vocation, and who, for that reason, deserve to be acknowledged.

First place belongs, of course, to my wife, Diane, and my children Hannah, Lydia, Ethan, and Adam. They are more precious to me than any earthly possession or honor. Possessing them, I am rich indeed. They truly believe in me, which is all that any man could ask of his family.

Next, the folks at Highland Books have been a joy to work with. George Grant's confidence in my scholarship has challenged me to transcend mediocrity; Heather Armstrong's buoyant spirit makes my deadlines less deadly; and Kathy Dempsey's editorial expertise gives me the reassurance that my sins will not find me out.

I also owe special thanks to my staff: the Rev. Tim Ward and his godly wife, Kim; David and Katherine Volz; Jim and Cathy Cummings; and Bryan and Deborah Short. Each of these friends is a sterling example of fidelity and service. Their contribution to my life and work will only be fully appreciated in the light of eternity, when every man will receive his due reward.

Other friends who have strongly encouraged me this past year are Wayne and Carolyn Carson and Rob and Karen Graham. Both of these families were simply "there" when, and if, my wife and I needed them. No questions or condemnation, just good old-fashioned love—the kind that shelters a friend from the harsher elements of life without asking for anything in return.

I would be remiss not to mention a few other special people who have had a profound influence on me: Harold Hendrick, for one, is one of the finest Christian gentlemen I have ever had the honor to know and work with. He is a leader worthy of emulation, and has by his example taught me much about graciousness and humility. Ken Shultz is another friend to whom I will forever be indebted. Ken has always showed me an extra measure of grace even when I did not deserve it, and continues to bless me with his optimism. And Dave Wilson supports and cheers me with his generosity and humor.

Special thanks to my siblings, Veronica Vaughan, Victoria Shipp, Jerry Vaughan, and Mark Vaughan, for all their positive words to their "little brother" the "author." And lastly, I have to mention my mother, Rosemary Werner Vaughan, who passed away while this book was being written. Though our loss is great, her gain is greater. We look forward to embracing her again in the land where tears and sorrow are no more.

PILLARS OF LEADERSHIP

INTRODUCTION
The Literature of Leadership

Books on leadership are often as majestically useless as they are pretentious.[1]

*E*ven a superficial perusal of the many books on leadership reveals that a majority of them fall into a few basic categories. The most common, perhaps, is the business-leader genre. These books discuss the concept of leadership within the framework of the modern corporation and use the language of market strategies and corporate hierarchical structures. Written for people in upper-management (or those who would like to be there), business-leader books attempt to inspire the "mere manager" to be a corporate leader and thus increase the productivity of the company. Indeed, in this category of leadership books, the bottom line is often better performance, which means measurable output for the sake of nothing nobler than corporate profits.

Next to books on corporate leadership, political leadership continues to hold a prominent place in the literature of leadership. In fact, it is fair to say that the study of political leadership has the longest literary tradition when compared to books on other types of leadership. Over 2,500 years ago philosophers of both East and West were giving serious thought to the question of what constituted a good ruler and how such leaders could be developed. From the East we have Sun Tzu's classic *The Art of War* as well as the *Analects* of Confucius; and from the West, or more properly the Mediterranean, we have inherited perhaps the most famous ancient text on politics, *The Republic* of Plato. Old as these texts may be, they continue to hold a fascination for those interested in the fine art of leadership.[2]

Ambitious clergymen can also find a plethora of books exhorting them to spiritual leadership or pastoral success. Using Biblical themes and examples, as well as anecdotes from parish life and pastoral experience, these volumes focus on the personal and devotional life of the pastor-leader, or offer advice on how to develop a "thriving" ministry or a "successful" (read "bigger") church. Serious books on pastoral theology have by and large given way to trendy books on "effective" strategies, thus showing the degree to which the business model of leadership has invaded the church.[3] With the burgeoning men's movement in Evangelical circles, there are now also scores of popular books on the meaning of manhood, leadership in the home, and moral and spiritual character development.

And, of course, there seems to be no end to secular self-help books and how-to books on personal enrichment. While awash in pop psychology and the rhetoric of personal improvement, the goal of these books is nearly always some form of material success, such as health or wealth.

Just as leadership literature falls into several basic categories, it also falls into a couple of basic errors. First of all, much of it is overly analytical or theoretical. This is especially true of many business-leader books. Although intended to distinguish the "mere" manager and the inspiring leader, much of this literature reduces leadership to a set of techniques which are the essence of managerial thinking, and thus is anything but inspiring. Whatever leadership is (and there is no agreement on that point), surely it must be something more profound than the slick application of technique.

Another error common to much leadership literature is narrow focus. In other words, leadership is defined and understood in the context of a specific occupation—say politics or business. But what works in one calling may not work in another. The corporate paradigm, for instance, has very limited application to the parish church, and when techniques or practices that work in one environment are imported into a foreign one, the results may be disastrous. Viewing leadership solely within the context of a given profession inevitably impoverishes our understanding of leadership itself.

What is needed, then, is a view of leadership that transcends mere technique and narrow focus. A view that is general but not vague, inspiring but not idealistic. Indeed, there is always the danger of swinging to either of two extremes: trivialization or romanticism. In the former, leadership is reduced to technique; in the latter it is enlarged to fiction. Yet it is neither. Real leadership is both ordinary and extraordinary. It is ordinary people doing extraordinary feats, as well as extraordinary people living ordinary lives.

In a word, leadership is life, and can never be abstracted from it. The same Churchill, for instance, who rallied England to "never give in" to the attacks of Nazi Germany, was also the same man who could weep over a maudlin movie or fawn over his household pets. And the same Patrick Henry who emboldened the fledgling American colonies to fight against the tyranny of the world's greatest military power, was also the same man who loved to roam the woods with a flintlock or entertain his children with a fiddle.

The simple and the heroic, the tedious and the triumphant, meet in one place: the soul of man. And the soul, as theologians tell us, is indivisible. Thus, while we may talk of leadership traits, and theorize about techniques or strategies, the essence of leadership lies in the realm of the inscrutable. Therefore, there is a sense in which leadership will always be a mystery. That does not mean, however, that we cannot or should not learn about it. It only means that we need less analysis and theory and more observation and inspiration. We need to not simply study leadership; we need to see it, to taste it, and to touch it.

And therein lies the value of the biographical approach to leadership. By looking at the lives of those who have gone before us, we learn that mere mortals, with flaws much like our own, can overcome enemies both within and without, and become exceptional leaders who make an important contribution to their world. Great men are not perfect; they are merely great. And their greatness is neither mythical nor unattainable. What makes them great is their triumph over the temptations and trials common to every man. Thus, great leadership is inspiring because it gives us hope—the hope that comes from knowing that others have faced our trials and endured, battled our demons and triumphed. And if they have been victorious, so can we.

THE NATURE OF LEADERSHIP

Life is a leaf of paper white
Whereon each one of us may write
His word or two, and then comes night.
Greatly begin! Though thou have time
But for a line, be that sublime—
Not failure, but low aim, is crime.[4]

The future is taking shape now in our own beliefs and in the
courage of our leaders. Ideas and leadership—not natural or social
"forces"— are the prime movers in human affairs.[5]

Consider your origins, you were not made to live as brutes,
but to follow virtue and knowledge.[6]

Only a sweet and virtuous soul,
Like season'd timber, never gives;
But though the whole world turn to coal,
Then chiefly lives.[7]

PROLOGUE

*Heroism is the brilliant triumph of the soul over the flesh: that is to say, over fear;
fear of poverty, of suffering, of calumny, of sickness, of isolation, and of death.*[8]

*I*n the spring of 1775, the American colonies were in crisis. In response to the Boston Tea Party the previous year, in which a band of American patriots boarded the British *Gaspee* and destroyed her cargo of tea, the British parliament closed the port of Boston and placed the city under martial law. The citizenry, however, is defiant.

In Virginia the delegates to the Convention are anxiously heading for Richmond to discuss the escalating crisis. Upon their arrival on March 20, the delegation is moved to St. John's Church in Henrico Parish, the only building large enough to hold the 120 delegates. It is a sultry day, so the windows of the church are opened and crowds gather outside straining to hear the proceedings. As roll is taken, they hear the names of such American notables as Thomas Jefferson, George Washington, James Madison, and Patrick Henry, to name only a few.

After the preliminaries, the atmosphere at the Convention turns gravely serious. Independence from Britain is the unspoken and explosive question on everyone's mind. Is it now time to fight? Should we arm the militia? Or should we consider further petitions? Can the stripling American colonies stand a chance against the British super-power? What of foreign alliances? Will France or Holland come to our aid? Is this rebellion or lawful resistance to tyranny?

For two days the questions are debated vehemently, yet the delegates remain unresolved. There is no decisive voice—no clarion call to action.

Patrick Henry then takes the floor. With a determination and courage characteristic of all great leaders, Henry addresses his distressed colleagues.

*No man, Mr. President, thinks more highly than I do of the
patriotism, as well as the abilities, of the very honorable gentlemen*

who have just addressed the House. But different men often see the same subject in different lights; and, therefore, I hope it will not be thought disrespectful to those gentlemen if, entertaining, as I do, opinions of a character very opposite to theirs, I should speak forth my sentiments freely, and without reserve. This is no time for ceremony. The question before the house is one of awful moment to this country. For my own part, I consider it as nothing less than a question of freedom or slavery. And in proportion to the magnitude of the subject ought to be the freedom of the debate. It is only in this way that we can hope to arrive at truth, and fulfill the great responsibility which we hold to God and our country. Should I keep back my opinions at such a time, through fear of giving offense, I should consider myself as guilty of treason towards my country, and of an act of disloyalty towards the majesty of Heaven, which I revere above all earthly kings.

Mr. President, it is natural to man to indulge in the illusions of Hope. We are apt to shut our eyes against a painful truth, and listen to the song of that siren till she transforms us into beasts. Is this the part of wise men, engaged in a great and arduous struggle for liberty? Are we disposed to be of the number of those who, having eyes, see not, and having ears, hear not, the things which so nearly concern their temporal salvation? For my part, whatever anguish of spirit it may cost, I am willing to know the whole truth; to know the worst, and to provide for it.

I have but one lamp by which my feet are guided, and that is the lamp of experience. I know of no way of judging the future but by the past. And, judging by the past, I wish to know what there has been in the conduct of the British ministry, for the last ten years, to justify those hopes with which gentlemen have been pleased to solace themselves and the House. Is it that insidious smile with which our petition has been lately received? Trust it not, sir; it will prove a snare to your feet. Suffer not yourselves to be betrayed with a kiss. Ask yourselves how this gracious reception of our petition comports with those warlike preparations which cover our waters and darken our land. Are fleets and armies necessary to a

work of love and reconciliation? Have we shown ourselves
so unwilling to be reconciled, that force must be called in to win
back our love? Let us not deceive ourselves, sir. These are the
implements of war and subjugation,—the last arguments to which
kings resort.

I ask gentlemen, sir, what means this martial array, if its purpose
be not to force us to submission? Can gentlemen assign any other
possible motive for it? Has Great Britain any enemy in this quarter
of the world, to call for all this accumulation of navies and
armies? No, sir, she has none. They are meant for us: they can be
meant for no other. They are sent over to bind and rivet upon us
those chains which the British ministry have been so long forging.

And what have we to oppose to them? Shall we try argument? Sir,
we have been trying that for the last ten years. Have we anything
new to offer upon the subject? Nothing. We have held the subject
up in every light of which it is capable; but it has been all in vain.
Shall we resort to entreaty, and humble supplication? What terms
shall we find which have not been already exhausted?

Let us not, I beseech you, sir, deceive ourselves longer. Sir, we have
done everything that could be done to avert the storm which is
now coming on. We have petitioned; we have remonstrated; we
have supplicated; we have prostrated ourselves before the throne,
and have implored its interposition to arrest the tyrannical hands
of the ministry and Parliament. Our petitions have been slighted;
our remonstrances have produced additional violence and insult;
our supplications have been disregarded; and we have been spurned
with contempt from the foot of the throne.

In vain, after these things, may we indulge the fond hope of peace
and reconciliation. There is no longer any room for hope. If we
wish to be free; if we mean to preserve inviolate those inestimable
privileges for which we have been so long contending; if we mean
not basely to abandon the noble struggle in which we have been
so long engaged, and which we have pledged ourselves never to

abandon until the glorious object of our contest be obtained,—we must fight! I repeat it, sir,—we must fight! An appeal to arms, and to the God of hosts, is all that is left us.

They tell us, sir, that we are weak,—unable to cope with so formidable an adversary. But when shall we be stronger? Will it be the next week, or the next year? Will it be when we are totally disarmed, and when a British guard shall be stationed in every house? Shall we gather strength by irresolution and inaction? Shall we acquire the means of effectual resistance by lying supinely on our backs, and hugging the delusive phantom of Hope, until our enemies shall have bound us hand and foot?

Sir, we are not weak, if we make a proper use of those means which the God of nature hath placed in our power. Three millions of people armed in the holy cause of liberty, and in such a country as that which we possess, are invincible by any force which our enemy can send against us.

Besides, sir, we shall not fight our battles alone. There is a just God who presides over the destinies of nations, and who will raise up friends to fight our battles for us. The battle, sir, is not to the strong alone: it is to the vigilant, the active, the brave. Besides, sir, we have no election. If we were base enough to desire it, it is now too late to retire from the contest. There is no retreat but in submission and slavery. Our chains are forged. Their clanking may be heard on the plains of Boston. The war is inevitable. And let it come! I repeat it, sir, let it come!

It is in vain, sir, to extenuate the matter. Gentlemen may cry peace, peace, but there is no peace. The war is actually begun. The next gale that sweeps from the north will bring to our ears the clash of resounding arms. Our brethren are already in the field. Why stand we here idle? What is it that gentlemen wish?

What would they have? Is life so dear, or peace so sweet, as to be purchased at the price of chains and slavery? Forbid it, Almighty God! I know not what course others may take, but as for me, give me liberty, or give me death! [9]

As we now know from our history texts, the Colonies declared their separation from Britain, fought and won the War of Independence, established a new Republic and framed a new Constitution—all the work of a small group of leaders.

The crisis they faced, however, was far graver than the threat of political subjection or military defeat. It was a crisis of will—the will to do the right thing though costly; the will to pursue the righteous path though painful; the will to act on principle though tempted to timidity. Would they lead the nation into freedom, or would they simply talk about liberty? Would they engage the enemy with courage or accommodate him with cowardice? Would they stand on principle or fall back on policy? Would they be leaders or followers?

In effect, our Founding Fathers were facing a crisis of leadership. Britain may have been the enemy, but the crisis was within themselves. For since it is a country's leaders who ultimately determine the fate of the nation, every social crisis is, at a deeper level, a crisis of leadership.

CRISIS IN LEADERSHIP

When ancient opinions and rules of life are taken away, the loss cannot possibly be estimated. From that moment, we have no compass to govern us, nor can we know distinctly to what port we steer. [10]

In order to appreciate today's leadership dearth, recall that when the American colonies joined together to form the United States, they numbered approximately three million persons. Yet out of that small population there arose an astounding number of local, national, and international leaders—men such as Samuel Adams, George Washington, Thomas Jefferson, Benjamin Rush, Patrick Henry, and others. And in Britain, of course, there were such admirable leaders as Pitt, Fox, Burke, and Wilberforce, just to name a few.

With today's American population of 240 million we might be expected to produce eighty times as many world-class leaders. [11] But we have not. On the contrary, it seems as if today there is an increasing awareness that we are a nation in crisis. As Ted Engstrom has stated:

> *Our nation and world today are faced with problems that appear insurmountable. Security and defense problems are staggering. For the most part, our youth, our future leaders, are confused, alienated, and demoralized. . . Moral standards are almost nonexistent. The growing national debt, bankrupt nations, financially troubled cities, and economic instability create more alarm each passing day.* [12]

Yet these problems, argues Engstrom, are only symptomatic of a deeper crisis—the crisis in leadership. "These crises, and many others, stem first from a lack of positive, constructive, dynamic, creative leadership." [13]

Others would agree. For instance, leadership gurus Warren Bennis and Burt Nanus state:

> *The need was never so great. A chronic crisis of governance— that is, the pervasive incapacity of organizations to cope with the expectations of their constituents—is now an overwhelming factor worldwide. If there was ever a moment in history when a comprehensive strategic view of leadership was needed, not just by a few leaders in high office but by large numbers of leaders in every job. . . it is now.*[14]

Author Donald Krause concurs, "Understanding the nature of leadership and developing strong leadership skills is probably the single most important task for society today."[15]

Why is leadership so important, you might ask? Because, as Krause rightly notes, "organizations and nations prosper or decline based solely on the vision and capability of their leaders."[16] It is as simple as that. So why, in contrast to our founding era, are we failing to produce first-class leadership?

One reason is what popular author Leanne Payne calls the "crisis in masculinity." This malady, which afflicts so many men in our society, is a crisis of identity in which men fail to understand and live out their gifts and calling as men. It is a condition, says Payne, in which men are seriously "split off" from their masculine side and identity, with the result that many men remain immature and passive with regard to their role as leaders. They "lose to one degree or another the power to act as father, husband, and leader."[17]

Moreover, we are experiencing a crisis in masculinity because there has been an ongoing decline of the role of the father in both the family and society. As David Blankenhorn has ably demonstrated in his ground breaking book, *Fatherless America,* "as paternity is decultured, the larger meaning of masculinity in our society becomes unclear and divisive. A decultured fatherhood thus produces a doubtful manhood."[18] Here is the operative phrase, "a doubtful manhood"—the lack of male confidence so needed in leaders. Blankenhorn then continues, "For without norms of effective paternity to anchor masculinity, the male project itself is increasingly called into question and even disrepute."[19]

The result of a decultured fatherhood and doubtful manhood is a generation of men who are insecure, aimless, narcissistic, and increasingly violent—just the opposite of those qualities needed in a leader. Says Blankenhorn:

> In social terms, the primary results of decultured paternity are a decline in children's well-being and a rise in male violence, especially against women. In a larger sense the most significant result is our society's steady fragmentation into atomized individuals, isolated from one another and estranged from the aspirations and realities of common membership in a family, a community, a nation, bound by mutual commitment and shared memory.[20]

Therefore, the crisis in masculinity is a reflection of the current decay of the family, especially the increasing failure of fatherhood, since it is the father who passes on to his son the true meaning of manhood and leadership. This is not to say, however, that a fatherless individual is doomed to a life of mediocrity or failure. Churchill, for example, is a notable example of a man who was mistreated by his father, and yet became a great world-class leader. The problem in our day is not that there is a growing minority of fatherless individuals; rather, "we are losing something larger: our idea of fatherhood."[21] And along with it we are losing our idea of manhood and leadership.

In addition to the crises of manhood and fatherhood, other modern forces war against the development of genuine leaders. Radical feminism, of course, abhors the notion of patriarchy, or male leadership, and socialism continues its assault against the family. But beneath both these and other modern "isms" we are really suffering a widespread crisis of meaning. As Solzhenitsyn told a stunned Harvard audience, the problem in the West is that "Men have forgotten God."[22] And once God and the idea of transcendent and absolute truth were abandoned, moral relativism rushed in to fill the void.

Moral relativism, however, can never produce genuine leaders. For at the heart of relativism is the denial of morality—of things like virtue, honesty, and integrity. And where there is no virtue, there can be no leadership, no inspiration to greatness, no vision for a noble life. In a word, the world of relativism is a world without heroes: no heroes to remember, no heroes to become. "Anti-heroism, denying traditional faith, offers neither a new vision of good to move men nor the courage of leadership. It cannot, in a word, summon the heroic resources that are the true determinants of human affairs."[23]

If the essence of leadership is moral excellence, as I believe, then moral relativism will never produce anything but mediocrity at best, and tyranny at worst. We cannot challenge young men to moral greatness when we have made the very notion obsolete. This was C.S. Lewis' observation over a generation ago. When he reviewed some texts that were being used in the British school system, Lewis found that the trend was to "debunk" the very idea of an objective standard of morality while still expecting young men to be virtuous—an impossible task. As Lewis so memorably put it:

> *And all the time—such is the tragi-comedy of our situation—we continue to clamour for those very qualities we are rendering impossible. You can hardly open a periodical without coming across the statement that what our civilization needs is more "drive," or dynamism, or self-sacrifice, or "creativity." In a sort of ghastly simplicity we remove the organ and demand the function. We make men without chests and expect of them virtue and enterprise. We laugh at honour and are shocked to find traitors in our midst. We castrate and bid the geldings be fruitful.[24]*

Thus today's paucity of leadership reflects the general decay in morality and meaning that always accompanies the rejection of God and moral absolutes.[25] The social milieu, if you will—home, church, and society—is the soil from which leadership springs. "Great men speak to us," says Will Durant, "only so far as we have ears and souls to hear them; only so far as we have *in us* the roots, at least, of that which flowers out in them."[26] Hence, a healthy society produces strong leaders: which is why our founding era produced such an astounding number of men of intellectual ability, moral strength, and sterling leadership.

But if social conditions are wrong, then the wrong type of leader—the charlatan or tyrant—more easily emerges. Moral anarchy and social chaos are always the underbelly of a violent volcano, ready to spew out a powerful and destructive force in the form of a charismatic but despotic leader. Chaos always calls forth control—anarchy yields tyranny. Thus the cavalier manner in which so many modern philosophers discard traditional morality is a blind invitation for oppression in the person of "the Leader." It is not surprising that our relativistic age, despite all its professed love of democracy and freedom, has seen more tyranny and bloodshed than any preceding age. "Spurning God, man becomes subject to the power and torments of genocidal dictators; trading freedom for security he gets neither, only a new slavery; rejecting absolute standards, he is victimized by absolute evil."[27]

With our very society at stake, it behooves us to discern the true meaning of leadership.

DISCERNING
TRUE LEADERSHIP

The world is not perishing for the want of clever or talented or well-meaning men.
It is perishing for the want of men of courage and resolution who, in devotion to
the cause of right and truth, can rise above personal feeling and private ambition.[28]

*T*he current crisis in leadership, with the threat it poses to social stability and personal happiness, demands that we understand the true nature of leadership. Defining the essence of leadership is no easy task, however, seeing that there is really no agreed upon definition. According to James MacGregor Burns, who authored the Nobel prize-winning book *Leadership,* there are at least 130 current definitions of leadership;[29] while Bennis and Nanus claim there are at least 350.

> *Decades of academic analysis have given us more than 350*
> *definitions of leadership. Literally thousands of empirical*
> *investigations of leaders have been conducted in the last seventy-*
> *five years alone, but no clear and unequivocal understanding*
> *exists as to what distinguishes leaders from non-leaders,*
> *and perhaps more important, what distinguishes* effective
> *leaders from* ineffective *leaders and* effective *organizations from*
> ineffective *organizations.*[30]

Indeed, Donald Krause was right when he said that the very subject of leadership "is a controversial topic that has spawned many theories about what constitutes capable leadership. . ."[31] Consider some of the following definitions.

Leadership is influence. That's it. Nothing more; nothing less.[32]
What is leadership? Remove for a moment the moral issues behind
it, and there is only one definition: Leadership is the ability to
obtain followers.[33]

We have conceived of leadership. . . as the tapping of existing and
potential motive and power bases of followers by leaders, for the
purpose of achieving an intended change.[34]

Though leadership may be hard to define, the one characteristic
common to all leaders is the ability to make things happen. . .[35]

Leadership can be defined as the will to control events, the
understanding to chart a course, and the power to get a job done,
cooperatively using the skill and abilities of other people.[36]

Leadership is a dynamic process in which a man or woman with
God-given capacity influences a specific group of God's people
toward His purposes for the group.[37]

Leaders are careful risk-takers, diligent and tireless workers,
occasional rule-breakers, empowerers and guiding forces for the
people around them, goal-setting questors, and skilled and
charismatic communicators.[38]

Leadership appears to be the art of getting others to want to
do something you are convinced should be done.[39]

Leadership is the ability to get men to do what they don't want to
do and like it.[40]

At the root of many of these definitions is the idea that leadership can be reduced to sheer influence. The leader is the mover and the shaker; he makes it happen; he gets things done. The popularity of this idea is reflected in the fact that Dale Carnegie's book *How to Win Friends and Influence People* has sold nearly fifteen million copies worldwide.

Although it is true that leaders influence their followers, influence is less the essence of leadership than it is one of its by-products. But more importantly, by reducing leadership to mere influence there is always the danger of confusing leadership with manipulation, and thereby viewing people as things. Burns aptly describes the pernicious effect of the Carnegie-type "how-to" manuals:

> While few of them today emulate the master in offering Machiavellian advice on how to coerce, control, or deceive other persons, many do seek to train persons to manage and manipulate other persons rather than lead them. The technique is usually that of the marketplace manipulation: to play on low-order wants and needs and to create hopes and aspirations where none existed before, through the use of saturation, promotion, and propaganda. Worse, the manuals treat persons as things, as tools to be used or objects to be stormed like a castle. At best they search for the lowest common denominator of motives among persons and within persons and exploit those motives for the benefit of the power wielder, not the target.[41]

The sad result of the "how to influence" school of leadership is that leadership is reduced to a salesman's bag of tricks: how to get your foot in the door, how to create desire, how to close the sale—hardly a noble view of leadership.

Another common but erroneous notion of leadership is to equate it with "success." Success, of course, is always defined in material terms such as the acquisition of power, position, or wealth; and those who have these things are accorded celebrity status. Gawking at "The Lives of the Rich and Famous" we become enamored with the trappings of attainment, forgetting that internal greatness and external advantage are as distinguishable as a man and his clothing. "A man's life," said Jesus, "does not consist in the abundance of the things that he possesses."[42] It takes only a moment's reflection to realize that many men have acquired wealth by unscrupulous means, and that scoundrels have attained notoriety. Wealth and fame tell us nothing about a person's character. This is especially true today when the media can, by the sheer force of its ubiquitous presence and technological wizardry, create a virtual reality studded with stars and celebrities.

Nevertheless, many Evangelicals, who are supposed to be "in the world but not of it," have been molded by the media culture that surrounds them, thereby succumbing to the "celebrity fallacy." Instead of desiring great leaders, says Calvin Miller, we often "admire superstar believers."

> *We evangelicals often elevate our superstars to idol status. We gape at them and hunger for their autographs. Why? Because they are great leaders? No! Because they give us a feeling of touching greatness with none of the demands that great leaders endure. We elevate them to marquis status because they flatter us in allowing us to know them while they require nothing of us. We sometimes create non-content neurotics by our adulation, knowing that it is a lot easier to live with stars than leaders.*[43]

Bedazzled by the bright lights of Broadway and the awesome images of Hollywood, we are like little children who enthusiastically applaud the magician for creating illusions—except in our case the illusion is a form of self-deception. The trick is on us, for our applause is an expression of self-flattery. Which is precisely why William James decried "the moral flabbiness born of the exclusive worship of the bitch-goddess success."[44]

As we shall see, true leadership is much more profound than either influence or advantage, though it may bring both. It is not primarily what a man does, but what he is—not his impact, but his character. As the proverb states, "Keep thy heart with all diligence; for out of it are the issues of life."[45] And so it is with leadership.

THE BASIC REQUIREMENT
OF LEADERSHIP

*Someone says: "The only thing that walks back from the tomb with
the mourners and refuses to be buried, is character." This is true.
What a man is, survives him. It never can be buried.* [46]

*T*he religious and political leaders who founded the United States spent countless hours in churches, town-halls, conventions, and legislatures hammering out the details of a constitutional republic—a system of government delicately balanced to minimize government power and maximize personal freedom. Their goal was ordered liberty: law without tyranny, liberty without license.

Yet as much as they labored over the drafting of our foundational legal documents, the Founders realized that good laws alone would never make a good society. The key to good government and a good society was good men—leaders of character. Thus, it was their studied opinion that the basic requirement of leadership is virtue.

For instance, the authors of *The Federalist* stated:

> *The aim of every political constitution is or ought to be first to
> obtain for rulers men who possess most wisdom to discern, and
> most virtue to pursue, the common good of the society; and in the
> next place, to take the most effectual precautions for keeping them
> virtuous, whilst they continue to hold their public trust.* [47]

And in the Virginia ratification debate, Patrick Henry declared:

I go on this great republican principle, that the people will have
virtue and intelligence to select men of virtue and wisdom. . .
To suppose that any form of government will secure liberty or
happiness without any virtue in the people, is a chimerical idea.[48]

But what exactly did America's founders mean by virtue? And how does it relate to leadership?

The idea of virtue has a long genealogy in the literature of the West, and the founders' notion of it was a product of their classical training and Christian faith. From the ancients, most notably Plato, they inherited what came to be called the "classical" or "cardinal" virtues—wisdom, justice, temperance, and courage. Aristotle associated these with other virtues such as prudence, magnanimity, liberality, and gentleness.[49] The Romans of the early Christian era accepted this Greek formulation and frequently spoke of the necessity of virtue in leaders. For instance, Cicero says in his *Republic*:

What can be more noble than the government of the state by
virtue? For then the man who rules others is not himself a slave to
any passion, but has already acquired for himself all those qualities
to which he is training and summoning his fellows. Such a man
imposes no laws upon the people that he does not obey himself, but
puts his own life before his fellow-citizens as their law.[50]

With the advent of Christianity, the cardinal virtues were supplemented by the "theological" virtues taught by St. Paul—faith, hope, and charity—the latter meaning primarily love for God.[51] It was Aquinas who officially baptized the previously pagan virtues into the Christian tradition and demonstrated their compatibility with right reason.

For the formal principle of the virtue of which we speak is good as
defined by reason; which good can be considered in two ways.
First, as existing in the very act of reason: and thus we have one
principal virtue, called Prudence [practical wisdom]. Secondly,

according as the reason puts its order into something else; either into operations, and then we have Justice; or into passions, and then we need two virtues. For the need of putting the order of reason into the passions is due to their thwarting reason: and this occurs in two ways. First, by the passions inciting to something against reason; and then the passions need a curb, which we call Temperance [moderation, self-control]. Secondly, by the passions withdrawing us from following the dictate of reason, e.g., through fear of danger or toil: and then man needs to be strengthened for that which reason dictates, lest he turn back; and to this end there is Fortitude [courage].[52]

The four cardinal virtues and the three theological virtues constituted the Seven Virtues of the Scholastics, to which they opposed the Seven Deadly Sins: pride, avarice, lust, anger, gluttony, envy, and sloth. The Middle Ages, in turn, were transformed by this idea of virtue. It became the "chivalric ideal"—the necessary traits of a "knight" or noble leader. For example, Díaz De Gámez could write in the fifteenth century:

What is required of a good knight? That he should be noble. What means noble and nobility? That the heart should be governed by the virtues. By what virtues? By the four [cardinal virtues] I have already named. These four virtues are sisters and so bound up one with the other, that he who has one, has all, and he who lacks one, lacks the others also. So the virtuous knight should be wary and prudent, just in the doing of justice, continent and temperate, enduring and courageous; and withal he must have great faith in God, hope at His glory, that he may attain the guerdon of the good that he has done, and finally he must have charity [love for God] and the love of his neighbour.[53]

Throughout the Renaissance and Reformation no one doubted the reality and necessity of virtue. Dante said it was virtue that distinguished men from brute beasts,[54] while Shakespeare saw it as the power of conscience, that "will plead like angels, trumpet-tongu'd."[55] The great Elizabethan poet Spenser enshrined virtue in his *Faerie Queene,* and the Protestant poet and polemicist, John Milton, taught that the end of all knowledge was the acquisition of virtue and faith. He said in his treatise on education:

> *The end then of learning is to repair the ruins of our first parents by regaining to know God aright, and out of that knowledge to love him, to imitate him, to be like him, as we may the nearest by possessing our souls of true virtue, which, being united to the heavenly grace of faith, makes up the highest perfection.*[56]

By the time of America's founding, the traditional idea of virtue was firmly rooted in the thinking and philosophy of the West. For the founders, therefore, religion and morality—the Christian virtues and the cardinal virtues—were inseparable from one another; and, more importantly, inseparable from good government and just leadership. In his famous *Farewell Address,* George Washington urged his countrymen to look well to the religious and moral foundations of free government.

> *Of all the dispositions and habits, which lead to political prosperity, Religion and Morality are indispensable supports. In vain would that man claim the tribute of Patriotism, who should labor to subvert these great pillars of human happiness, these firmest props of the duties of Men and Citizens. . . And let us with caution indulge the supposition, that morality can be maintained without religion. Whatever may be conceded to the influence of refined education on minds of peculiar structure—reason and experience both forbid us to expect, that national morality can prevail in exclusion of religious principle.*

> *Tis substantially true, that virtue or morality is a necessary spring of popular government. The rule indeed extends with more or less force to every species of Free Government. Who that is a sincere*

friend to it can look with indifference upon attempts to shake the foundation of the fabric?[57]

As a public figure, a leader was "one who towered above his fellow citizens, a person in whom courage, wisdom, self-restraint, and just dealing were conspicuous."[58] Or, as historian Forrest McDonald put it, the American ideal of public virtue "entailed firmness, courage, endurance, industry, frugal living, strength, and above all unremitting devotion to the weal of the public's corporate self, the community of virtuous men."[59]

Today we use the word "character" to mean that a man is basically "good" or "sound," much like the word "integrity" means soundness of principle and character. "A person with integrity does not have divided loyalties (that's duplicity), nor is he or she merely pretending (that's hypocrisy). People with integrity are 'whole' people; they can be identified by their single-mindedness."[60]

That is all true. But "virtue" is a more positive and energetic concept; and in its earlier use implied "the qualities of full humanity: strength, courage, capacity, worth, manliness, moral excellence."[61] Whereas "integrity" is a passive quality, "virtue" is an active one, suggesting moral energy. As Terry Glaspey notes, "Virtue is more than just the absence of vices. It is a powerful, positive force for good in our lives. As G.K. Chesterton once wrote, 'Virtue is not just the absence of vices or the avoidance of moral dangers; virtue is a vivid and separate thing'. . . Virtue is the ability and power to choose good. . ."[62]

To hold, as I do, to the traditional view of virtue is to repudiate the modern notion of relativism. As Gertrude Himmelfarb has argued we have traveled "from virtues to values," and the distance between the two is astronomical. The chasm cannot be bridged. Whereas for centuries "virtues" were thought to be objective and authoritative, now "values" are merely subjective and relative. It was Nietzche, she argues, who ushered in the revolution against the classical and Christian virtues. "The 'death of God' would mean the death of morality and the death of truth—above all, the truth of any morality. There would be no good and evil, no virtue and vice. There would be only 'values.'"[63]

In addition, now that we have reduced all moral questions to personal values, many persons suppose that the private and public lives of our leaders can somehow be divorced. As George Grant has accurately observed:

*We moderns hold to a strangely disjunctive view of the relation-
ship between life and work—thus enabling us to nonchalantly
separate a person's private character from his or her public accomplishments. But this novel divorce of root from fruit, however gen-
teel, is a ribald denial of one of the most basic truths in life: what
you are begets what you do; wrong-headed philosophies stem from
wrong-headed philosophers: sin does not just happen—it is sinners
that sin.*[64]

This attempt to separate the private and public, or the moral from the
practical, has produced disastrous consequences, because a man's character
inevitably affects his philosophy and policy. Bad men make bad decisions and
frame bad laws. That is why a leader's character is always the essential issue in
determining his fitness to govern. Noah Webster warned us of this over 200
years ago.

*When you become entitled to exercise the right of voting for public
officers, let it be impressed on your mind that God commands you to
choose for rulers, "just men who will rule in the fear of God." The
preservation of government depends on the faithful discharge of
this duty; if the citizens neglect their duty and place unprincipled
men in office, the government will soon be corrupted; laws will be
made, not for the public good so much as for selfish or local purposes; corrupt or incompetent men will be appointed to execute the
laws; the public revenues will be squandered on unworthy men; and
the rights of the citizens will be violated or disregarded.*[65]

Does all this sound familiar? Indeed it does. For we have forgotten that
character, or what I prefer to call virtue, is the first basic prerequisite of sound
leadership. Virtue (in the singular) is not simply one of many positive traits,
but the amalgam or sum total of the many qualities necessary for trustworthy
leadership, which is why it serves as its fundamental requirement. Without it a
man may be a great orator and persuader, as was Hitler, but he will never be a
great leader. He may be a man of intelligence and wit, as was Rousseau, but

he will never be a man of wisdom. He may be a man of incredible will and strength, as was Stalin, but he will never be a man of accomplishment.

It is moral excellence or virtue that ensures a leader will truly rule in the best interest of his followers. It is this quality of character that will keep him humble in popularity, restrained with power, and self-controlled amidst prosperity. And it is a leader's moral excellence that will give him moral authority with other men—the influence that comes not out of a bag of tricks but out of a soul of virtue.

THE KEYS TO INFLUENCE

A dogmatic belief in objective value is necessary to the very idea of a rule which is not tyranny or an obedience which is not slavery.[66]

I t is true that a leader influences his followers. Indeed, he could not *lead* them, properly speaking, if he did not influence them. But why should one man follow another? Indeed, why *do* people follow a leader, even when it may mean great sacrifice and peril to themselves?

Apart from situations that are coercive, people respond to a leader because they have a fundamental trust in, or respect for, that leader. As Robert Greenleaf suggests:

> *Every achievement starts with a goal—but not just any goal and not just anybody stating it. The one who states the goal must elicit trust, especially if it is a high risk or visionary goal, because those who follow are asked to accept the risk along with the leader. Leaders do not elicit trust unless one has confidence in their values and competence (including judgment) and unless they have a sustaining spirit (entheos) that will support the tenacious pursuit of a goal.*[67]

Thus the primary task of any aspiring leader is to become a person who is worthy of respect. What does this require?

First of all, it requires personal character development. As we have seen, a leader's influence is more than the application of gimmicks or techniques: it is the power of his character. The notion of virtue implies a moral energy—an energy not only to act, but an energy that acts upon others. It is, basically, the influence of moral excellence, which is perhaps better described as "moral authority." Moral excellence grants moral authority; or, in other words, integrity gains respect. "In order to be a leader," Eisenhower once said, "a man must have followers."

> *And to have followers, a man must have their confidence. Hence, the supreme quality for a leader is unquestionable integrity. Without it, no real success is possible. . . If a man's associates find him guilty of being phony, if they find that he lacks forthright integrity, he will fail. His teachings and actions must square with each other. The first great need, therefore, is integrity and high purpose.*[68]

Secondly, virtue suggests not only goodness but also competence. The virtuous man possesses the industry, fortitude, and wisdom that are the prerequisites for mastering any task or discipline. When a leader fully understands the subject under discussion, then he can speak with confidence and wisdom. People respect knowledge and ability, but will not follow the advice or orders of a man who is either uninformed or ill-equipped. On the other hand, "the more competent the other fellow knows you are," says William Oncken, Jr., the more "he will think of you as an authority in the matter under consideration and will feel it risky to ignore your wishes."[69] Mastery enhances authority.

Thirdly, a leader's authority is also a product of his personality. While it is true that there is no single leadership style or, as Peter Drucker says, no single "effective personality,"[70] it is also true that a leader's general demeanor must be respectable. In other words, he cannot be rude, opinionated, angry, or demeaning; but rather he should be prudent, fair, kind, and reasonable.[71] Any glaring flaw in a leader's personality will work to diminish his reputation in the eyes of others, and hence undermine his authority.

Fourthly, a leader's authority is partly a product of his position—his place in the organization or society to which he belongs. Although a man's position does not guarantee that others will respect him, his position can be a valuable aid in his exercise of leadership. Men do "salute the uniform" as it is said—they give deference to position even though they may not respect the man. A leader knows this and strives to see that he does not bring his office or position into disrepute. On the contrary, he uses his official influence to advance his program for the best interests of others. As Teddy Roosevelt employed his office of President, every leader can use his position as a "bully pulpit" to articulate his vision and chart a course for the future.[72]

Lastly, a leader's authority is directly related to his service toward others. The idea of servant-leadership has been with us for centuries, having permeated our everyday language; thus we can speak of politicians or policemen as "public servants." It originated, however, not in the halls of humanism but in the cradle of Christianity, even in the earthly example and teaching of Christ himself. For instance, when an ambitious mother of two of his followers approached Jesus, and requested that her sons be given positions of power in his kingdom, he answered:

> Ye know that the princes of the Gentiles exercise dominion over them, and they that are great exercise authority upon them.
>
> But it shall not be so among you: but whosoever will be great among you, let him be your minister; And whosoever will be chief among you, let him be your servant:
>
> Even as the Son of man came not to be ministered unto, but to minister, and to give his life a ransom for many.[73]

The principle of servant-leadership is, says Robert Greenleaf, that "which holds that the only authority deserving one's allegiance is that which is freely and knowingly granted by the led to the leader in response to, and in proportion to, the clearly evident servant stature of the leader." He continues:

> Those who choose to follow this principle will not casually accept the authority of existing institutions. Rather, they will freely respond only to individuals who are chosen as leaders because they are proven and trusted as servants. To the extent that this principle prevails in the future, the only truly viable institutions will be those that are predominantly servant-led.[74]

Genuine leadership, therefore, is not a matter of holding a powerful position or exercising coercive power over others. It is not a matter of issuing commands. It is not a matter of sitting in an impressive office devising plans and strategies and programs. It is not a matter of talk, which is cheap. Rather, real leadership is the expression of a life—a life of sacrifice in the service of others. "Sadly," laments George Grant, "all too many Christians have not comprehended this link between charity and authority. They have not understood that authority comes through service."[75]

But those who preach and don't practice are hollow leaders—in fact they are not leaders at all. For a leader not only says, "Do as I say," but more importantly, "Do as I *do*." He not only says, "Follow my orders," but more significantly, "Follow *me*." A leader cannot expect what he does not exemplify, nor demand what he does not do.

But when a man is imbued with the spirit of sacrificial service he will gain the loyalty and dedication of others. Sensing his humble but noble altruism—being willing to lay down his life for them—his followers will respond in kind. There is simply no substitute for service.

A true leader, therefore, exercises influence because he is a man of virtuous character, competent ability, and sacrificial service. His moral authority is both earned and deserved. Ultimately, as Teddy Roosevelt observed, a man's character is reflected in his deeds, and earns him the right to lead.

> *Before a man can discipline other men, he must demonstrate his ability to discipline himself. Before he may be allowed the command of commission, he must evidence command of character. Look then to the work of his hands. Hear the words of his mouth. By his fruit you shall know him.*[76]

LOOKING FORWARD
The Next Generation

For the wise men of old, the cardinal problem of human life was how to conform the soul to objective reality, and the solution was wisdom, self-discipline, and virtue. For the modern, the cardinal problem is how to conform reality to the wishes of man, and the solution is technique.[77]

When we recall that there are literally hundreds of possible definitions of leadership, it should come as no surprise to learn that there is no agreed upon method of developing leaders. The goal determines the means. Which is a simple way of saying that one's definition of leadership will influence, if not determine, one's view of leader education. Moreover, the field of endeavor, if you will, also shapes the content and focus of the training. For instance, the training received by military officers is different than that received by MBA students. And so it should be. Their organizations are different, their subjects are different, and their missions are different. So of course their training is different.

But are there no general principles of leadership development that can be discovered? Yes. But remember, presuppositions determine principles and practice. And in my view, the basic requirement of leadership is virtue or moral excellence. It is that fundamental quality of character that will express itself in many noble ways, such as determination, courage, and discipline, for example—in what I call the pillars of leadership. So, if virtue is the essential requisite of leadership, the paramount question then becomes, "Can virtue be taught?"

Russell Kirk in a perceptive essay of the same title asked that same question.[78] After surveying the traditional meaning of virtue, Kirk suggests that there is no simple prescription for learning the moral virtue necessary for leadership. Bennis agrees, "There is no simple formula, no rigorous science, no cookbook that leads inexorably to successful leadership. Instead, it is a deeply human process."[79] Or, as I would say, leadership is a function of the soul, and thus will always be partially veiled to human view.

Does that mean that virtue or leadership cannot be learned? No, it merely means that it will not be learned by commonly accepted forms of management training that take place in many universities. In fact, as Kirk claims, "moral virtue is not learnt in schools."[80] Not that schooling is unimportant, it is just that schools play only a subsidiary role to other institutions, most notably family. The best that schools can do is to function *in loco parentis,* which means that they must reinforce the values espoused by the parents. Unfortunately, the public schools of today often function *contra parentem,* undermining respect for parental authority and scorning the religious and moral teaching parents attempt to instill in their children. As a result they exacerbate the current crisis in leadership.

The family, then, is the place where all leadership training really begins. For in the context of the family good moral habits are acquired, values are shaped, and character is formed. Indeed, the importance of the family in determining character can hardly be overestimated, as Christopher Lasch argues:

> *As the chief agency of socialization, the family reproduces cultural patterns in the individual. It not only imparts ethical norms, providing the child with his first instruction in the prevailing social rules, it profoundly shapes his character, in ways of which he is not even aware. The family instills modes of thought and action that become habitual. Because of its enormous emotional influence, it colors all of a child's subsequent experience.*[81]

Lasch goes on to point out why schools are no match for the family when it comes to real education, which means the transmission of culture.

> *If the reproduction of culture were simply a matter of formal instruction and discipline, it could be left to the schools. But it*

also requires that culture be embedded in personality. Socialization
makes the individual want to do what he has to do; the
family is the agency to which society entrusts this complex
and delicate task.[82]

By saying that the family is primary in the development of character, and hence leadership, I am not saying that the place to begin is with the children. Instead, we must begin with the parents. It was Chesterton who wisely criticized the cry to "save the children," a common mantra of educators and bureaucrats, as "an evil cry." For by focusing on the children we forget the fathers. As Chesterton put it, "'Save the children' has in it the hateful implication that it is impossible to save the fathers; in other words, that many millions of grown up, sane, responsible and self-supporting Europeans are to be treated like dirt or debris and swept away out of the discussion. . ."[83]

However, without the parents, most notably the fathers, you cannot properly educate the children.

Now I am concerned, first and last, to maintain that unless you
can save the fathers, you cannot save the children; that at present
we cannot save others, for we cannot save ourselves. We cannot
teach citizenship if we are not citizens; we cannot free others if
we have forgotten the appetite of freedom. Education is only truth
in a state of transmission; and how can we pass on truth if it has
never come into our hand? . . .It is vain to save children; for they
cannot remain children. By hypothesis we are teaching them to be
men; and how can it be so simple to teach an ideal manhood to
others if it is so vain and hopeless to find one for ourselves?[84]

Consequently, any plan of leadership development must take into account the essential requisite of moral virtue and the primary place of the family; whereas any approach which tends to undermine the institution of the family or the authority of the father will eventually weaken our prospects for sound leaders in the future. The recovery of virtue in America depends "in great part upon the reinvigoration of family," says Kirk. "It would be vain for us to pretend that schools and colleges somehow could make amends for all the neglect of character resulting from the inadequacies of the American family of the 'Eighties and 'Nineties."[85]

Next to the family, the church has an important role to play in the recovery of virtue and the development of leaders. Established as "the pillar and ground of the truth" the church is called to expound and enforce the Scriptures, thereby bringing men to maturity and equipping them for "good works."[86] The original charter given to the church by Christ himself requires the church to "disciple the nations" and to "teach" the whole counsel of God.[87] In other words, the church is by its foundational charter an educational institution designed to produce men and women of moral excellence.

Commenting on the pedagogical role that the church plays in promoting virtue and leadership, George Grant points out:

> The church is to train God's people for the work of the ministry. If our nation is to have thoroughly equipped pastors, then the church must train young men for the ministry of the gospel. If our nation is to have thoroughly equipped teachers, then the church must train young mothers and fathers for the ministry of education. If our nation is to have thoroughly equipped craftsmen, artists, musicians, philosophers, doctors, laborers, lawyers, scientists, and merchants, then the church must train them for the ministry of acculturation. And, of course, if our nation is to have thoroughly equipped magistrates, then the church must train them for the ministry of cultural and political involvement.[88]

Russell Kirk agrees that the preaching ministry of the church plays a vital role in producing leaders. "Certainly there would be little virtue in our civilization, and quite possibly there would exist no modern civilization at all, were it not for Christian preaching of the theological virtues. From the discipline of the theological virtues issue saints from time to time, as from the discipline of the cardinal virtues issue heroes."[89]

The development of moral virtue is primarily a matter of habit and discipline. Virtue is acquired not so much by abstract instruction as by practical inculcation. Therefore, the family and the church will go a long way in providing institutional support for leadership development. Nevertheless, it would be wrong to conclude that leaders simply spring out of the societal soil with no effort of their own. On the contrary, neither the family nor the church can "produce" leaders in the strict sense of the word. People are not products; and leaders are not manufactured on an assembly line. Each person is peerless and has innate abilities and a unique personality. Without descending into the debate over whether leaders are "born or made," it is clear that God has given to each person particular gifts and aptitudes, and that each has temperamental tendencies. Some are by nature more gifted to lead.

Yet gifts alone do not make a leader. In addition to natural talents, leadership requires the assertion of individual will and vision. What a man does with his talents is more telling than the gifts themselves. That was the whole point of Christ's parable of the talents. While we can, and should, school ourselves and our children in the habits of moral virtue, no amount of "family values" or "Bible teaching" will make a leader of the man who does not aspire to leadership. The man himself—his will, his vision, his ambition—is ultimately the determining factor, from the human point of view, in whether or not he becomes a leader. Will he count the cost, and then pay the price, for greatness? There is absolutely no escaping this personal responsibility for achievement.

Nevertheless it still remains the duty of the present generation to provide inspiration for the next. The question is, then, how shall that be accomplished?

LOOKING BACK
On the Shoulders of Giants

*We are like dwarfs on the shoulders of giants, so that we can see more
than they, and things at a greater distance, not by virtue of any sharpness of
sight on our part, or any physical distinction, but because we are
carried high and raised up by their giant size.*[90]

One would think that modern moral relativism would spawn a respect and appreciation for the past. Surely if all "truths" are equally valid, then ideas and customs of preceding ages are worthy of our investigation and contemplation. In other words, "multiculturalism" should work backwards as well as sideways.

Yet it is one of the contradictions of relativism that on the contrary it yields a profound ignorance of the past. No, it is worse than that. It breeds a decided bias against the past, what David Hall calls "the arrogance of the modern,"[91] and C. S. Lewis terms "chronological snobbery:"[92] a hostile prejudice against the past based on the false notion that modern "progress" has made the past irrelevant to modern concerns. This arrogant snobbery has cut us off from the vast reservoir of ancient wisdom and knowledge so much needed amidst modernity's vapid public discourse.

But what, you might ask, does history have to do with leadership? Much in every way. Primarily, history holds the key to aspiration. In the form of biography, it provides a mighty catalyst that inspires young people to aspire to greatness. It is a spur to achievement. It provides models to emulate. It paints the colors and contours of virtue on the canvas of our imagination, thereby stimulating imitation.

Perhaps nobody better described the benefit of meditating on the character and achievements of earlier leaders, than the ancient historian Plutarch. In his *Parallel Lives,* he instructs us that when we read the lives of great men, their virtue produces in our minds "an emulation and eagerness that may lead. . . to imitation."[93] Why is this? Because virtue itself inspires.

It is a moral energy—"a practical stimulus"—that elicits the desire to act in a similarly noble fashion. As Plutarch put it:

> But virtue, by the bare statement of its actions, can so affect
> men's minds as to create at once both admiration of the things
> done and desire to imitate the doers of them. The goods of fortune
> we would possess and would enjoy; those of virtue we long to
> practice and exercise. We are content to receive the former from
> others, the latter we wish others to experience from us. Moral good
> is a practical stimulus; it is no sooner seen, than it inspires an
> impulse to practice, and influences the mind and character not by a
> mere imitation which we look at, but by the statement of the fact
> creates a moral purpose which we form.[94]

And it is this "moral purpose" to imitate which is at the heart of aspiration. Without it, all the talents and treasures of the potential leader lie dormant in the dust. But with it, men are challenged to greatness, and hence to true leadership. As Teddy Roosevelt once confessed, "From reading of the people I admired—ranging from the soldiers of Valley Forge and Morgan's riflemen to my Southern forefathers and kinfolk—I felt a great admiration for men who were fearless and who could hold their own in the world. And I had a great desire to be like them."[95] And what was true of Roosevelt was also true of other great leaders. Through the influence of history and biography they were inspired to emulate virtue. "A leader lives his life as a sincere imitator of the best attributes of others," says George Grant. "Heroes always have heroes."[96]

The power of virtue to stimulate emulation is partly due to the fact that imitation is a "law of our nature." As William Symington said over a century ago:

> The disposition to commemorate events, whether of public or
> private interest, springs from a law of our nature. . . Matters
> of great and permanent utility, the due consideration of which is
> fitted to exert a continued beneficial influence on society, are thus
> held forth to the view of the community, and prevented from

passing into oblivion. The very act of reminiscence itself is calculated to call into operation, and consequently to improve by exercising, some of the higher moral principles of the heart, such as gratitude for benefits received, veneration for departed worth, and imitation of praiseworthy excellence.[97]

Since imitation is natural, our young people will search for, and find, examples to copy. The urgent question is, therefore, who shall serve as models? The drugged rock stars and corrupt celebrities of the present, or the noble leaders and virtuous examples of the past? With so few reliable role models in the present (for it seems that nearly every would-be example has a skeleton in his closet) why not mine the rich resources of past achievement and valor? Why be impoverished by a meager modernity, when we can be enriched by a prosperous past? Why not hold before our eyes, and the eyes of our children, images of courage, and duty, and faith, and sacrifice that have passed the test of historical scrutiny? In short, why stumble over pygmies when we can stand upon giants?

Of course, the anti-heroism of our age is opposed to this biographical approach to leadership, and seems bent on dispelling the "myth" of great men. By highlighting the flaws and failures of past leaders, the "new biography" attempts to discredit the public virtues of great men by revealing their private vices. In the process the biographer himself, by cutting his subject down to size and showing that he was, after all, a mere man, becomes the new hero. This is what is now termed "pathography—a biography emphasizing the pathological or diseased qualities of the subject. . ."[98] At the root of this new approach to history and biography is the envious denial of eminence and the nihilistic denial of "the very idea of individuality."[99] It is relativism come home to roost. With no moral absolutes there can be no such thing as virtue or greatness; and with no transcendent Creator, men are nothing more than helpless victims to historical causes.

In response to the new history, it is only necessary to quote Himmelfarb who wryly commented, "An ingenious historian can always find ways of eluding reality."[100]

We are not so naive as to think that yesterday's leaders were perfect. They were not. Each one was subject, as are we, to the fatal flaw of original sin. So, to discover their failings takes no talent at all. C. S. Lewis observed that a critic is always a second-rate man. It takes no virtue to discover vice. But it does take virtue to emulate virtue. Criticism is easy; accomplishment is hard.

Nobody said it better than Theodore Roosevelt:

> *It is not the critic that counts; not the man who points out how the strong man stumbles, or where the doer of deeds could have done better. The credit belongs to the man who is actually in the arena, whose face is marred by dust and sweat and blood; who strives valiantly, who errs, and comes short again and again, because there is no effort without error and shortcoming; but who does actually strive to do the deeds.*[101]

As we look at the character of former leaders, we should liken our quest to a treasure hunt not a witch-hunt. We seek gold not dross. But if we must dig through the ore to find the gold, then we are so much the better for our labor. The riches we will unearth are worth the effort—and our emulation.

THE PILLARS OF LEADERSHIP

It is only when we can transport ourselves to the distant past and evoke from its obscurity the forms of its heroic men: it is only when we acquaint ourselves with the errors they combated, the difficulties they surmounted, the hardships they endured, that we can fully comprehend the character of the men who thus toiled and suffered, or appreciate their value.[102]

Every great nation owes to the men whose lives have formed part of its greatness not merely the material effect of what they did, not merely the laws they placed upon the statute books or the victories they won over armed foes, but also the immense but indefinable moral influence produced by their deeds and words themselves upon the national character.[103]

Great men are the ambassadors of Providence sent to reveal to their fellow men their unknown selves. . . When the reverence of this great nation for its great men dies, the glory of the nation will die with it.[104]

A desire to know intimately those illustrious personages, who have performed a conspicuous part on the great theatre of the world, is, perhaps, implanted in every human bosom.[105]

CHRISTOPHER COLUMBUS
(1451–1506)

Born Cristoforo Colombo in Genoa, Italy, Columbus was the eldest of five children. The son of a wool weaver, he had little formal education and appeared destined to follow his father's humble trade.

Columbus took to the sea, however, when only ten years old, and through experience and self-education acquired a masterly knowledge of mathematics, astronomy, geography, cosmography, history, and classical literature. As a result of his reading, reflection and interaction with seamen and scholars, Columbus became convinced that the Indies could be reached by sailing west. After presenting his "enterprise of the Indies" to John II, King of Portugal, and being rebuffed, Columbus turned to Isabella I, Queen of Castile in 1486. Intrigued by the idea, the Queen retained Columbus on a pension while her royal advisers considered the plan. It was not until January of 1492 that Isabella and Ferdinand granted Columbus the necessary papers and finances to pursue his dream.

Thus on August 3, 1492, the three caravels—the Niña, the Pinta, and the Santa María launched out on their historic expedition manned with eighty-eight seamen. Backed by providentially good winds, the caravels sailed west along the twenty-eighth parallel, quickened toward their unknown destination. After a near mutiny, land was sighted on October 12 at 2:00 am. That day Columbus landed on an island in the Bahamas, which he christened San Salvador (Holy Savior). After exploring Haiti, Columbus established the colony of La Navidad (The Nativity) and then returned to Spain triumphant.

During the next eleven years, he made three more voyages in which he either discovered or explored the West Indies, the Virgin Islands, Puerto Rico, Trinidad, the Gulf of Paria, Martinique, Honduras, and Panama. It was in Panama that he learned of the vast ocean that was only a few days march across the mountains.

Although Columbus never reached the Indies, he did discover a "new world" to be claimed not merely for Isabella, but for Christendom. And his faith, courage, and sense of divine mission that fueled his daring exploits earned him the title of "Admiral of the Ocean Sea."

FAITH

Jesus said that all things would pass away, but not His marvelous Word.
He also affirmed that it was necessary that all things be fulfilled that were
prophesied by Himself and by the prophets. Thus, I hold alone to the
sacred and holy Scriptures.[106]

I n 1492 Columbus sailed the ocean blue—and the rest, as they say, is history.

Not exactly—for as it turns out, the discipline of history, like the actual history it records, is not stagnant. Due to the shifts of time and place, Columbus is either famous or infamous depending on one's ideological perspective. Indeed, many modern historians now regard Columbus' achievements not as exploits, but as exploitation: at his feet have been laid the full blame for all of the interracial cruelty and intrigue that followed in the wake of his discovery of the new world.[107]

While it is true that much injustice was done to the original tribes who welcomed Columbus and his sailors to the New World, Columbus himself is hardly to blame for the avarice, cowardliness, and lust of others. Yet modern historians insist on painting him as a greedy, inhumane villain. Why? Because Columbus has come to represent more than the adventurous spirit of the Renaissance—the age of discovery; rather, he now symbolizes the hopes and dreams of Christendom. Modern historians recognize this, even if only intuitively, and smell the scent of Christianity, which to them is not a fragrance but a stench.

And their intuitions are correct, for Columbus was a man of deep religious faith who believed in the Scriptures, the Church, and the Crusades. He was no gold-hungry Conquistador, no adventure-loving Musketeer, no self-seeking Higaldo. No, he was a true believer: a man who thoroughly imbibed the spirit of Christendom into which he was born.

Accordingly, Columbus was throughout his life a man of strict personal piety. As his contemporary biographer, Las Casas, described him:

*He observed the fasts of the church most faithfully, confessed
and made communion often, read the canonical offices like a
churchman or member of a religious order, hated blasphemy and
profane swearing, was most devoted to our Lady and to the
seraphic father St. Francis; seemed very grateful to God for
benefits received from the divine hand, wherefore, as in the
proverb, he hourly admitted that God had conferred upon him
great mercies, as upon David.[108]*

His son, Ferdinand, who also wrote a biography of his father, concurs with this evaluation of Columbus' piety. "In matters of religion he was so strict that for fasting and saying all the canonical offices he might have been taken for a member of a religious order."[109]

Thus it is not surprising that, from beginning to end, the journey to the New World was marked with devout expressions of the Christian faith. For instance, on the morning of August 3, 1492, Columbus, having received his commission from Isabella, knelt on the dock to receive Holy Communion before launching out toward the Indies.[110] And daily on the ships the men would recite the *Pater Noster* and chant the *Ave Maria,* each dawn being greeted with singing:

*Blessed be the light of day
and the Holy Cross, we say;
and the Lord of Veritie,
and the Holy Trinity.*

*Blessed be th' immortal soul,
and the Lord who keeps it whole,
Blessed be the light of day,
and He who sends the night away.[111]*

To pass the time on the long trip, the seamen would regularly invoke the well-known prayer *Dios Nos:*

*Give us good days, good passage, and good company; so let there
be good voyage. Thus, days on end, may God grant your graces,
gentlemen of the afterguard and gentlemen of the forward.*[112]

In response to prayers such as these, the *Niña,* the *Pinta,* and the *Santa
María* enjoyed unusually fair weather and good speed. Throughout the entire
journey they did not even encounter one troubling storm. Winds and weather
wafted them to their destination as if God Himself was filling their sails with
His breath/For men who many times had battled the raging sea for their very
lives, such fair sailing was a token that God had indeed heard their prayers and
was granting them providential passage.

On October 12 at 2:00 am, a cry was heard from the *Pinta,* "Tierra!
Tierra!" At long last—after seventy-two days at sea—and after hours of prayer
and supplication, the faith of Columbus was vindicated. At daybreak he,
followed by the Pinzón brothers and a small retinue, waded toward the shore
as their boats lingered outside the dangerous shoal. Columbus was the first to
set foot on dry ground. After planting the royal standard bearing the crest of
Ferdinand and Isabella, the men kissed the burning white beach. Knowing
that God had given them success, they knelt and prayed with tears streaming
down their faces:

*O Lord, Almighty and everlasting God, by Thy holy Word Thou
hast created the heaven, and the earth, and the sea; blessed and
glorified be Thy Name, and praised be Thy Majesty, which hath
deigned to use us, Thy humble servants, that Thy holy Name may
be proclaimed in this second part of the earth.*[113]

Columbus then christened the island San Salvador—"Holy Saviour."

As the men sang, danced, prayed, and celebrated they were being spied
upon by phantom figures hiding in the lush foliage. Slowly, one by one, the
timid natives stepped out from nature's shadow on to the shore. Columbus
was impressed by their handsome appearance and kind manners, and offered
them small tokens as a sign of good will. He did this, he said, "In order that we

might win good friendship, because I knew that they were a people who could better be freed and converted to our Holy Faith by love than by force."[114]

On another occasion, Columbus had a conversation with a native ruler about "the sundry journeys and rewards of souls departed from their bodies," and informed the ruler that "the chief cause of his coming thither was to instruct them in such godly knowledge and true religion, and that he was sent into those countries by the Christian King of Spain (his lord and master) for the same purpose."[115] Biographer Las Casas confirms Columbus's concern for the salvation of the Indians; "He was extraordinarily zealous for the divine service; he desired and was eager for the conversion of these people [the Indians], and that in every region the faith of Jesus Christ be planted and enhanced."[116]

Columbus, then, had a far nobler vision than mere self-aggrandizement, although he was not immune to the inducements of rank, honor, and even profit. Like all true leaders, his faith birthed within him a vision for doing good and grand services for his fellow man. Modern historians may have difficulty believing this, but that is only because they have difficulty with faith itself. They simply cannot relate to the hidden workings of faith and do not understand that a man like Columbus—indeed, any man—may actually walk with God.

Nevertheless, Columbus' faith in God that is the invisible key to unlocking the mystery of his achievements. As Morison so well said:

> Always with God, though; in that his biographers were right;
> for God is with men who for a good cause put their trust in Him.
> Men may doubt this, but there can be no doubt that the faith
> of Columbus was genuine and sincere, and that his frequent
> communion with forces unseen was a vital element in his
> achievement. It gave him confidence in his destiny, assurance
> that his performance would be equal to the promise of his name.[117]

PROVIDENCE

No man should fear to undertake any task in the name of our Saviour, if it is just and if the intention is purely for His holy service. The working out of all things has been assigned to each person by our Lord, but it all happens according to His sovereign will even though He gives advice. He lacks nothing that it is in the power of men to give him. Oh what a gracious Lord, who desires that people should perform for Him those things for which He holds Himself responsible![118]

I t has been called by many names—providence, destiny, fate, and even fortune. Yet in reality, it is the invisible hand of God guiding the course of history. For Columbus it meant being called to fulfill a divine mission and having the assurance of divine aid in times of need. Living in light of divine destiny gave Columbus confidence, hope, and courage.

As with other great leaders, destiny made its mark early; so early that Columbus was not even aware at the time of God's providential dealing in his life. When only an infant, his parents, Dominico and Susanna, fortuitously christened him Christopher—"Christ Bearer"—after the patron saint of travelers. Christopher's name became his destiny.

The story of Saint Christopher, which was familiar to every child in the Middle Ages, tells of a pagan who heard the story of Christ and went off in search of Him. Inquiring of a hermit where he might find Christ, the holy man said, "Perhaps Our Lord will show Himself to you if you fast and pray." Christopher replied, "Fast I cannot, and how to pray I know not; ask me something easier." So the hermit asked him, "Knowest thou that river without a bridge which can only be crossed at great peril of drowning?" "I do," said Christopher. "Very well," replied the hermit, "take up thine abode by the hither bank, and assist poor travelers to cross; that will be very agreeable to Our Lord, and perhaps He will show Himself to thee."

So Christopher obediently complied with the hermit's instructions and built a cabin by the riverbank where there was no bridge or boat to carry the wayfarers across. Instead, with the aid of a tree trunk for a staff, Christopher would carry the travelers through the water on his shoulders.

One night while Christopher was asleep in his humble hut, he was awakened by the voice of a small child. "Christopher! Come and set me across." With staff in hand, Christopher took the infant on his shoulders and made way through the water. But as he waded through the river the child's weight so increased as to become nearly intolerable—as if he were carrying the entire weight of the world on his back. He called forth all his strength and, with the aid of his staff, struggled to the other bank.

"Well now," said Christopher to his passenger, "thou hast put me in great danger, for thy burden waxed so great that had I borne the whole world on my back, it could have weighed no more than thou."

"Marvel not, Christopher," replied the child, "for thou hast borne upon thy back the whole world and Him who created it. I am the Christ whom thou servest in doing good. As proof of my words, plant your staff by your cabin, and in the morning it shall be covered with blossoms and fruit." Saint Christopher did as he was told, and on the morrow it was so.[119]

This simple legend, intended to teach the Catholic doctrine that Christ could be found in the way of good works, had a profound influence on Columbus. He genuinely believed that like his patron saint, it was his mission—his divine destiny—to carry Christ and his Gospel across the waters of the great western ocean. According to Morison:

> He conceived it his destiny to carry the divine word of that
> Holy Child across the mighty ocean to countries steeped in
> heathen darkness. Many years elapsed and countless
> discouragements were surmounted before anyone would
> afford him means to take up the burden. Once assumed, it
> often became intolerable, and often he staggered under it; but
> never did he set it down until his appointed work was done.
> We may fairly say that the first step toward the discovery of
> America was taken by the parents of Columbus when they
> caused him to be baptized Cristoforo. . .[120]

Columbus' faith in the legend and the providential meaning of his name is evident in the manner in which he recorded his signature. Of the nearly fifty documents that have preserved his signature, his name always appears as follows:

$$S$$
$$S \cdot A \cdot S$$
$$X \, M \, T$$
$$:Xpo \; Ferens$$

This enigmatic inscription has aroused endless speculation, but the most simple and reasonable is this:

Servus
Sum Altissimi Salvatoris
Christi Maria Yesu
:Xpo Ferens,

which means in English—*Servant I am of the Most High Saviour; Christ, Mary, Jesus (or Joseph): the Christ Bearer.* Thus Columbus saw himself as the servant of God who was predestined to be a witness for Christ; indeed, to bear Christ across the water as did his patron saint. His signature was a reminder, therefore, "that by baptism he was consecrated to the task of carrying the word of God overseas to heathen lands."[121]

While the legend of Saint Christopher, and Columbus' faith in his own divine mission, may strike the modern reader as "medieval" or even childish, there is no doubt that his faith in providence was a major key to his motivation and success. "This conviction that God destined him to be an instrument for spreading the faith was far more potent than the desire to win glory, wealth, and worldly honors. . ." notes biographer Morison.[122] Indeed, Daniel Boorstin comments, "It was his divinely appointed errand to enlarge the realm of the True Faith with the souls of pagan millions. His confidence as God's messenger had given him strength to bear years of ridicule and to risk mutiny."[123]

True enough indeed; for it was Columbus' faith in God's providential calling that lead him to study the Scriptures for guidance, to presume upon the benefactions of royalty, to endure rejection and ridicule, to brave the unknown and uncharted seas, and to battle both hostile nature and hateful men. His childish faith bore manly fruit.

It is striking, and itself providential, that the oldest known map of Columbus' discoveries, drawn by his friend and shipmate Juan de la Cosa, is illuminated by the image of Saint Christopher bearing the infant Jesus on his shoulders.

Providence created a pious pioneer, and destiny marked his daring deeds.

VISION

*It was the Lord who put it in me to sail from here to the Indies. The fact that
the Gospel must be preached to so many lands—that is what convinced me.
Charting the seas is but a necessary requisite for the fulfillment of the
Great Commission of our glorious Savior.*[124]

V ision is an indispensable mark of true leadership; on this, all agree. And
there is no doubt that Columbus was a man with a vision; or as Morison
put it, a "man with a mission." So much so, that historian Daniel Boorstin has
noted Columbus' "single-minded devotion to his Enterprise of the Indies,"[125]
and has labeled his vision to reach the Indies a "monomaniacal project."[126]
Washington Irving, the well-known biographer of Columbus, has also noted
his "uncommon" sense of vision:

> *His conduct was characterized by the grandeur of his views and
> the magnanimity of his spirit. Instead of ravaging the newly
> found countries, he sought to colonize and cultivate them, to
> civilize the natives. He had a valiant and indignant spirit
> and an ardent and enthusiastic imagination. He was a visionary
> of uncommon kind.*[127]

But what exactly was Columbus after? The Indies, no doubt, but why? Was
it gold, glory, or the gospel? In other words, was Columbus an enterprising
entrepreneur or a Christian crusader? And how did he come up with the idea
of landing in the east by sailing west?

As an experienced seaman, Columbus had traveled southward along the
African coast and eastward along all of the established trade routes of the
Mediterranean. He joined expeditions to Guinea, the Azores, the Canaries,
Madeira, Cape Verde, and Porto Santo. But he also traveled northward,
visiting London, Bristol, Galway, and eventually Iceland. And it was here

that Columbus heard with fascination the tales of the Scandinavian Norsemen, most notably Eric the Red, who discovered Greenland, Labrador, Nova Scotia, and mainland Canada, which was called Vinland. Was this a new continent? Most Europeans thought not; rather they held that the Vikings had merely stumbled upon the northern limit of the Eurasian continental landmass, Ultima Thule. Yet Columbus wondered. . .

He began to collect evidence. For instance, Martin Vicente, who was a pilot for the Portuguese crown, told Columbus that he had found a finely carved piece of wood when sailing four hundred leagues west of Cape St. Vincent. Pedro Correa, also in the employ of Portugal, gave similar testimony, as did King Joao. Columbus also heard reports from several reliable seamen that winds from the west had left pine branches, strange driftwood, and on one occasion, the bodies of two tawny-skinned men who were washed ashore at Flores. Other seamen reported sightings of unknown islands in the uncharted west and strange dugout boats floating at sea.[128]

Columbus also began to read. For instance, he read Ptolemy's *Geography* in order to estimate the size of the earth, and Plutarch's *Lives* to gain noble inspiration and observe providence. One of the books that most influenced Columbus' opinion of the feasibility of sailing west was *Imago Mundi,* a world geography written about 1410 by the French theologian-astrologer Pierre d'Ailly. Here Columbus found strong evidence that his enterprise was possible. In his own copy, which is heavily annotated and underlined, he found the following telling statement:

> *The length of the [Eurasian] land toward the Orient is much greater than Ptolemy admits. . . because the length of the habitable Earth on the side of the Orient is more that half the circuit of the globe. For, according to the philosophers and Pliny, the ocean which stretches between the extremity of further Spain (that is, Morocco) and the eastern edge of India is of no great width. For it is evident that this sea is navigable in a very few days if the wind be fair. . .[129]*

In addition, Columbus read and was influenced by Pope Pius II's *Historia Rerum Ubique Gestarum,* Joachim de Fiore's *Commentaries on Isaiah and*

Jeremiah, Marco Polo's *Milione,* John Mandeville's *Travels,* and other works. The one book that influenced Columbus more than any other, however, was the Bible. In his own work, the *Book of Prophecies,* Columbus pointed to the Bible as the source of his vision to sail to the Indies.

> *It was the Lord who put into my mind (I could feel His hand upon me) the fact that it would be possible to sail from here to the Indies. All who heard of my project rejected it with laughter, ridiculing me. There is no question that the inspiration was from the Holy Spirit, because he comforted me with rays of marvelous illumination from the Holy Scriptures, a strong and clear testimony from the 44 books of the Old Testament, from the four Gospels, and from the 23 Epistles of the blessed Apostles, encouraging me continually to press forward; and without ceasing for a moment they now encourage me to make haste.[130]*

Columbus likewise believed he found in the Scriptures that the Indies, or uttermost parts of the earth, not only *could* be discovered, but that they *ought* to be discovered. His design, he would later reveal, was to provide resources for a new Crusade and to spread the Gospel throughout the New World. From the beginning of his petitions for royal support, Columbus made his vision clear. For instance, he wrote, "At the time I was motivated by the Scriptures to go to discover the Indies, I went to the royal court with the intention of entreating our Sovereigns to specify revenues that they might accrue to be spent on the reconquest of Jerusalem."[131]

In a letter to Isabella, Columbus credited the Scriptures as the source of his crusading ardor, "The argument I have for the restitution of the Temple Mount to the Holy Church is simple: I only hold fast to the Holy Scriptures and to the prophetic citations attributed to certain holy men who were carried along by divine wisdom."[132] And to Pope Alexander VI he expressed his determination to recover the Holy Land, "The enterprise must be undertaken in order to spend any profits therein for the redemption of the Sepulchre and the Temple Mount unto the Holy Church."[133]

But what of gold? Wasn't Columbus really just a greedy adventurer bent on profit by plunder? No, he was not. As we learn from his numerous writings,

Columbus was seeking gold in order to fund a Crusade and win converts to Christianity. "Gold is most excellent," he exclaimed. But for what end? "Gold constitutes treasure, and he who possesses it may do what he will in the world, and may so attain as to bring souls to Paradise."[134]

During the first voyage he kept a journal which he intended to give to Ferdinand and Isabella. On December 26, 1492, he made an entry that shows his real motivation for discovering gold.

> *I hope to God that when I come back here from Castile. . . that I will find a barrel of gold, for which these people I am leaving will have traded, and that they will have found the gold mine. . . [so] that within three years the Sovereigns will prepare for and undertake the reconquest of the Holy Land. I have already petitioned Your Highnesses to see that all profits of this, my enterprise, should be spent on the conquest of Jerusalem . . .*[135]

The enterprise to the Indies, then, was driven by desire to gain revenues to fund a Crusade. Moreover, as a man of vision, Columbus saw an opportunity to fulfill the Great Commission of Christ to "disciple the nations, baptizing them in the name of the Father, Son, and Holy Spirit, teaching them to observe all that I have commanded you."[136] He genuinely believed that God had sent him to the Indies for His glory and the salvation of mankind, as he noted in his *Journal:*

> *And Your Highnesses will command a city and fortress to be built in these parts, and these countries converted. . . And I say Your Highnesses ought not to consent that any foreigner do business or set foot herein, except Christian Catholics, since this was the end and the beginning of the enterprise, that it should be for the enhancement and glory of the Christian religion, nor should anyone who is not a good Christian come to these parts.*[137]

Here, in the New World, Christianity would see its greatest triumphs—that was the vision of Columbus—a vision that merged into a prophecy. "And Your Highnesses will win these lands, which are an Other World *(que son otro mundo),* and where Christianity will have so much enjoyment, and our faith in time so great an increase."[138]

"Marvelous prophecy, superb faith!" says historian Morison.[139] And he is right. For at the time barely a handful of important people in Spain believed in the Enterprise. Yet as a man of vision, Columbus dared to go where others feared to tread, and foretold the eventual Christian colonization of the New World.

PATRICK HENRY
(1733–1799)

Patrick Henry was one of America's most powerful and popular patriots. Born in Hanover County, Virginia, Henry was raised in a religious home and sat for many years under the preaching of Samuel Davies, the father of American Presbyterianism.

Henry married early, and after a series of personal setbacks, entered the legal profession. He first gained notoriety as an orator when he pled the "Parson's Cause," in which he challenged the right of the King to annul colonial laws and to levy taxes without representation.

Henry was admitted to the Virginia House of Burgesses in 1765 and shocked the established aristocracy by boldly denouncing the Crown's recently passed Stamp Act. His defiant Stamp Act Resolutions began the ball of the Revolution rolling. He helped to organize the Committees on Correspondence, and during the Second Virginia Convention, gave his now famous "Give Me Liberty" speech, which propelled Virginia to arm itself against Britain. He was also a member of the First and Second Continental Congress.

After Virginia declared its independence in June of 1776, Henry was elected its first governor, and held that office for three consecutive terms (1776–1779) and was later reelected for two more terms (1784–1785). In the intervening years he was the leading politician in Virginia.

Henry declined his election to the Constitutional Convention in Philadelphia in 1787, and during the Ratification Convention in Virginia in 1788, he led the Anti-Federalists who opposed the Constitution in its unamended form. Although unable to halt ratification, Henry did succeed in seeing that a bill of rights was eventually added to the Constitution.

During the last years of his life, Henry refused such prestigious positions as U.S. Ambassador, Secretary of State, and Chief Justice of the Supreme Court; choosing rather to practice law and provide an inheritance for his family. In response to a personal appeal from Washington, Henry again ran for office in 1799 and was elected to the Virginia legislature. He died, however, before taking his seat.

ORATORY

Should I keep back my opinions through fear of giving offense, I should consider myself as guilty of treason towards my country and an act of disloyalty toward the majesty of Heaven, which I revere above all earthly kings.[140]

I f there is one thing for which Patrick Henry has been remembered, it is his spellbinding and moving oratory. More than anything else, his fame has come to rest on his spoken word, most notably his well-known exclamation "Give me liberty or give me death!" which is still memorized by thousands of American school children. Yet even in his own lifetime Henry's commanding eloquence was legendary, earning him such epithets as "the forest-born Demosthenes," the "Trumpet of the Revolution," and the "Son of Thunder."

All those who heard Henry deliver a public speech agreed that he was the most eloquent speaker in the Colonies, and probably the greatest orator in the Western world. Thomas Jefferson, for instance, said that Henry "spoke as Homer wrote," and that he was "the greatest orator that ever lived."[141] Edmund Randolph, another of Henry's contemporaries and political foes, gave Henry the highest tribute when he stated his belief that "for grand impressions in the defense of liberty, the Western world has not yet been able to exhibit a rival."[142] Coming from his political opponents, these are very high compliments indeed.

Even men who were themselves recognized as excellent orators "accorded to Mr. Henry the palm of oratory over all other men." For instance, John Randolph of Roanoke, who heard Henry in the *British Debt Case,* and who later earned the reputation as being one of the most eloquent speakers of his day, said that Henry was "the greatest orator that ever lived." On one occasion, when Randolph was asked to describe Henry's oratory, he picked up a piece of charcoal from a fireplace, pointed to a white wall and said:

> *But it is in vain for me to attempt to describe the oratory of that wonderful man. Sir, it would be as vain for me to try, with this black coal, to paint correctly the brilliant flash of the vivid lightning, or to attempt, with my feeble voice, to echo the thunder, as to convey, by any power I possess, a proper idea of the eloquence of Patrick Henry!*

Randolph declared that Henry, in sum, "was a Shakespeare and Garrick combined, and spake as never man spake."[143]

Considering these glowing testimonies, it is unfortunate that we do not have more records of Henry's excellent speeches. But one of the reasons that so few of his speeches have survived intact is that his eloquence was so spellbinding that often the House recorder forgot to take notes because he was enthralled with Henry's speech—indeed too captivated to write it down! According to the Reverend Conrad Speece, who witnessed Henry plead a criminal trial, when Henry spoke "my feelings underwent an instant change." Amongst the gallery there was an unusual "bowing of the soul." "The spell of the magician was upon us," said Speece, "and we stood like statues around him."[144]

Indeed, when Henry spoke it was not uncommon for his listeners to be so enraptured by his rhetoric that they would forget their surroundings. For instance, Judge Roane tells of a humorous incident involving his father.

> *It is among the first things I can remember, that my father paid the expenses of a Scotch tutor residing in his family, named Bradfute, a man of learning, to go with him to Williamsburg to hear Patrick Henry speak; and that he laughed at Bradfute, on his return, for having been so much enchanted with his eloquence as to have unconsciously spirited tobacco juice from the gallery on the heads of the members, and to have nearly fallen from the gallery into the House.*[145]

How do we account for the almost magical power of Henry's eloquence? First, he was a naturally gifted speaker, although this was not apparent when he was a young boy. Not until he pled the "Parson's Cause" did anyone who knew him—even his father—realize Henry's latent powers as an orator. Secondly, Henry had the good fortune of sitting under the preaching of Samuel Davies, who many considered the best preacher in the Colonies next to Whitefield. "It indeed seemed that God had given Patrick a superlative tutor and mentor in oratory during his formative years."[146]

Moreover, Henry's keen observation and deep reflection enhanced his natural gifts and early experiences. As a boy, he was really not much of a talker; rather, he liked to listen to others. Colonel Meredith once observed that Henry's habit in his boyhood was to attentively observe everything that occurred near him. "Nothing escaped his notice." This penchant for observation gave Henry deep insight into human nature. "He knew well all the springs and motives of human action." Thus, when he addressed a jury or assembly, "he measured and gauged them by a discriminating judgment," knowing how to produce the desired effect on their minds and hearts.[147]

But most importantly, Henry had power as an orator because he was sincere and earnest in his delivery. He meant what he said. And when he believed something deeply, he spoke it vehemently. While the written word can never do justice to the power of the spoken word, the following eyewitness account of Henry's delivery of his Liberty Speech gives us a glimpse into the secret of his power:

> Henry arose with an unearthly fire burning in his eye. He commenced somewhat calmly—but the smothered excitement began more and more to play upon his features and thrill in the tones of his voice. The tendons of his neck stood out white and rigid like whipcords. His voice rose louder and louder, until the walls of the building and all within them seemed to shake and rock in its tremendous vibrations. Finally his pale face and glaring eyes became terrible to look upon. Men leaned forward in their seats with their heads strained forward, their faces pale and their eyes glaring like the speaker's. His last exclamation—"give me liberty or give me death"—was like the shout of the leader which turns back the rout of battle![148]

Dr. Archibald Alexander, the president of Princeton Theological Seminary, once related that he went to hear Henry speak in order to "ascertain the true secret of his power." His conclusion was that "the power of Henry's eloquence was due, first, to the greatness of his emotion and passion. . ."[149]

Like all great leaders, Henry was a man of profound conviction; and because he was also a man of courage, he was not afraid to speak his mind. To "keep back my opinions," he said at St. John's, "through fear of giving offense," would be treason to his country and disloyalty to God. Henry's courage and conviction, therefore, was the true key to his oratorical power over men. And though few leaders will be able to imitate Henry's natural gifts as an orator, all may emulate the passion and conviction that set them ablaze.

POWER

*The experience of the world teaches me the jeopardy
of giving enormous power.*[150]

*T*he measure of a man's character can be gauged by how he handles success and power. While there are trials peculiar to adversity, there are temptations perilous in prosperity. Some amount of failure and adversity is the lot of every man—as it was to Henry. But not every man experiences the heights of popularity and power that he achieved. And how a man uses his position of influence says as much, if not more, about his character, than how he responds to struggles and setbacks. If he overcomes the trials of adversity, he must face the even greater trials of success.

After enduring a series of business and financial disappointments as a young man, Henry persevered and became a successful lawyer, businessman, and politician. With his successful and eloquent performance in the "Parson's Cause," he began a long and lucrative career as a defense attorney. As a general rule, he successfully defended most of his clients and never lacked customers eager for his services. His legal practice, however, was interrupted by his service in the Virginia Assembly, especially with the onset of the war.

As a result, Henry augmented his income by engaging in land speculation. Henry had a shrewd business sense (probably the product of his earlier financial failures), and throughout his life invested in promising land adventures. From 1768 to 1799, he was involved in land investments and plantation acquisitions, all made with an acute business intuition. Throughout this period of thirty-two years, Henry "owned at one time or another about one hundred thousand acres, and from 1789 to 1795 was a partner in a western land investment company that claimed what one author estimated to be fifteen and one-half million acres!" As an owner, speculator and trader, Henry turned the soil into profits, and before his death he was one of the wealthiest landowners in Virginia.[151]

His greatest success, of course, was as a political orator and statesman. Due to his spellbinding and splendorous eloquence, Henry was immensely popular with the mass of Virginians. He was virtually their "idol"—a celebrity before the cult of celebrities became a phenomenon. And after his Stamp Act Resolutions were published throughout the Colonies, America was filled with his fame.

But Henry's power and influence was not limited to the average citizen. For virtually his entire political career, he was the undisputed leader of the Virginia legislature. This fact is all the more striking when we remember that his colleagues numbered such men as George Washington, Thomas Jefferson, James Monroe, James Madison, and John Marshall—just to name a few. But whatever might be the individual or combined talents of his colleagues, Mr. Henry was easily the leader. . ."[152] For instance, after the Constitution was ratified, Henry returned to the Virginia Assembly sworn to see that it was amended to protect the people's liberty. Amidst the great legislative battle, he used his power and influence to essentially force Madison, then a United States Representative in Congress, to propose those amendments we now know as the "Bill of Rights." Washington, who was then President, feared Henry's "anti-Federal" disposition and wrote to Madison lamenting Henry's power over the Virginia House, "In one word it is said that the edicts of Mr. H are enregistered with less opposition in the Virginia Assembly than those of the grand monarch by his parliaments. He has only to say, 'Let this be law,' and it is law."[153] While perhaps an overstatement, it is nevertheless true that Henry was recognized by both political friend and foe as the unchallenged leader of Virginia—for many years the most powerful man in the state.

Ironically, Henry himself had a deep distrust of human power. Knowing the frailties of human nature, he well knew that power corrupts. Yet, surprisingly, Henry was remarkably free from abusing his own power and using his fame for personal advantage. On the contrary, he responded to popularity with humility and exercised power responsibly. Unlike so many leaders who become dizzy in the heights of prominence and power, Henry always kept his feet squarely planted on the ground. He was basically a modest man who could not be touched by fame. His character was his armor. Archibald Blair, a close friend of Henry, said of him, "I never saw anything tyrannical in his disposition, or otherwise ambitious than to be serviceable to mankind."[154] Moreover, Henry understood that power, especially political power, was a sacred trust to be used for the benefit of society. As one author said of Henry, "No man ever knew men better, singly or in mass; none ever better knew how to sway them; but none ever less abused that power; for he seems ever to have felt, with a religious force, the solemnity of all those public functions which so few now regard."[155]

We confuse the shadow for the substance when we imagine that fame and power are traits of a great leader. Fame has been given to fools, and power to tyrants. Rather, the real test of greatness is not whether a man possesses fame or power, but how he employs them. Henry was great, not because of power, but in spite of it. Being the great leader he was, he avoided the pitfalls of popularity—pride, egotism, and ingratitude—and did not fall from the pinnacle of power. He passed not only the test of failure, but the more trying test of success. And for that reason especially, he serves as a model for all those who aspire not to the shadow but to the substance of true leadership.

TRADITION

I call upon every gentleman here to declare, whether the king of England had any subjects so attached to his family and government—so loyal as we were. . . We retained from our earliest infancy, the most sincere regard and reverence for the mother country. Our partiality extended to a predilection for her customs, habits, manners and laws.[156]

A leader is a builder. Whether he is developing the character of his own children or expanding the markets of his business, he is building for the future. But instead of discarding the contribution of previous generations, a wise leader will always employ the resources and tools provided by the past as he constructs the future. In this sense, every great leader will be a traditionalist or conservative.

Surprising as it may sound, Patrick Henry was at heart a conservative, in spite of the fact that his ardent nature and bold speech earned him such labels as "radical" or "rebel," and that his early speeches were often met with shocked cries of "Treason!" His "radicalism," if it may be called that, "was radical only within the context of Virginia politics." Whereas Pendleton, Randolph, and others sought to maintain a long-standing working accommodation with royal authority, Henry pressed the Virginia leadership to take more decisive action against increasing royal interference. Nevertheless, Henry's political stance throughout the growing crisis with Britain was not a rejection of the English constitution per se, but rather a desire to see it "restored by purging it of corrupting influences."[157] The American "revolution," then was really a conservative movement aimed at preserving the existing social order from the external threat of British corruption.

If we take Russell Kirk's description of conservatism as our starting point,[158] it is clear that the "radical" Henry was a dyed-in-the-wool conservative. For instance, Henry believed in a transcendent moral order, which he referred to as "the law of nature." Being well acquainted with Vattel, Grotius, Montesquieu, and others, Henry accepted the notion that the law of nature and the law of God were essentially the same: the former recognized by reason and the latter perceived by faith. Henry's moral postulates were derived from the King James Version of the Bible and the Anglican catechism.

Second, Henry adhered to the conservative principle of "prescription," that is, "of things established by immemorial usage."[159] Although Henry was willing to propose, on occasion, novel legislation, he had a great respect for the long-standing British constitution, charters, and customs. More importantly he had a profound respect for "the experience of the world" and thus constantly consulted history as a guide. When reading Henry's speeches, one is impressed with the large number of historical illusions. For instance, in his Ratification speech, Henry repeatedly appealed to British history, Swedish history, Colonial history, and the history of other countries to defend his view.

Also, Henry was conservative in that he had a realistic view of human nature. As Kirk put it, "conservatives are chastened by their principle of imperfectability."[160] Henry believed that human nature was seriously flawed—it was fallen. And human depravity poses a very real threat to political liberty. "I dread the depravity of human nature," he told the Ratification Convention. "I will never depend on so slender a protector as the possibility of being represented by virtuous men."[161] Likewise, Henry's view of human nature led him to disavow any utopian social schemes. He did not believe in, nor attempt, simple and sweeping changes to society in order to usher in a humanists' paradise. He was a practical and prudent politician who had little faith in the theoretical psychology or abstract politics then seeping out of France. Thus, he criticized French skepticism and ultimately repudiated the French Revolution, which had as its object the destruction of everything, whether sacred or profane, that had gone before. "The spirit it developed was that of indiscriminate warfare on the past." The American Revolution, on the other hand, was a conservative, and even religious, movement. "The whole movement" of the revolution, one author has said, "had been eminently conservative and wise, following the suggestion of Bacon who says, 'It were good that men in their innovations, would follow the example of time, which indeed innovateth greatly, but quietly and by degrees.'"[162]

While Henry was a visionary, prophetic leader, he was rooted in what Kirk calls "the Great Tradition"[163]—the classical and Christian intellectual heritage that formed the curriculum of the schools and under-girded the existing social order. As a patriot, Henry's passion was preservation. He sought to protect the long-standing rights and liberties that he and his countrymen had enjoyed for decades—indeed, for centuries. Being rooted in the Great Tradition, Henry then hoped to build a future reflecting that tradition. As a wise leader, he was a master-builder erecting his edifice on the Foundation of the Great Tradition. And every sound leader-builder must do the same, or he will build on sinking sand.

WILLIAM WILBERFORCE

(1759–1833)

William Wilberforce, British philanthropist and statesman, is best known for his crusade to abolish slavery in the British Empire. He became a Member of Parliament for his hometown of Hull in 1780, and in 1784 was elected as MP for Yorkshire, a seat he retained until 1812, when he retired from Parliament.

Wilberforce was converted to Christianity in 1784–1785, and was the center of the Clapham Sect, a group of Evangelicals active in philanthropic and political causes. Wilberforce and the "Saints," as they were called, championed parliamentary reform, prison reform, and missionary endeavors, helping to establish the Church Missionary Society (1799), the British and Foreign Bible Society (1804), as well as other religious and charitable organizations.

Wilberforce's forty-year crusade against slavery saw its eventual abolition in 1833, and his influential book, A Practical View, *laid the foundation for the moral elevation of the Victorian Era that followed his death.*

PERSEVERANCE

God Almighty has set before me two great objects: the suppression of the slave trade and the reformation of manners.[164]

P erseverance is an outdated concept in our day of instant coffee, microwave meals, and computer quickness. Yet the difference between a dreamer's wish and a leader's accomplishment is often nothing more glamorous than plodding perseverance: the determination to continue working for the goal in spite of obstacles and setbacks, the will to win in the face of defeat and disappointment, the passion to press on when discouraged or discounted.

The leader who tenaciously pursues his objective is usually victorious over the man who may be more intelligent or gifted. As Calvin Coolidge rightly observed:

> *Nothing can take the place of persistence. Talent will not.*
> *Nothing is more common than unsuccessful men with talent.*
> *Genius will not. Unrewarded genius is almost a proverb.*
> *Education will not. The world is full of educated derelicts.*
> *Persistence and determination alone are overwhelmingly*
> *powerful."*[165]

As in Aesop's fable of the tortoise and the hare, perseverance wins the prize.

When William Wilberforce entered Parliament at the tender age of twenty-one he was ignorant of his actual calling in life. Like so many of his political colleagues, he saw his office as a means to personal advancement. However, in 1784–1785, Wilberforce traveled Europe with his mother, sister, and former schoolmaster—Isaac Milner. To pass the time, Wilberforce and Milner read Phillip Doddridge's classic, *The Rise and Progress of Religion in the Soul,* and discussed the New Testament as they road together in the coach. After a season of conviction and anguish, Wilberforce was converted.

For the next few years Wilberforce struggled with his vocation. What was God's will for him? Could he be both a worldly politician and a pious Christian? In desperation he visited the now-famous clergyman John Newton, who counseled him to stay in politics, believing that perhaps God would use him in that arena. Providentially, it was Newton, along with James Ramsey, Thomas Clarkson, and others, who influenced Wilberforce to take up the cause of the slaves.[166]

In 1787, as Wilberforce wrestled with God, he penned in his diary the conviction that God had called him to labor for the abolition of the slave trade. In light of his divine call, as well as the self-evident righteousness of his cause, Wilberforce expected a quick and easy victory. But he could not have been any more mistaken. "The pathway to abolition was fraught with difficulty. Vested interest, parliamentary filibustering, entrenched bigotry, international politics, slave unrest, personal sickness, and political fear—all combined to frustrate the movement." [167] Little did he know it would take twenty long and hard years of persistent effort to see his hope fulfilled.

Wilberforce began to press in Parliament the claims of the slaves in 1787. A year later, however, he fell seriously ill and had to postpone his efforts for a year. By 1789 he had recuperated and issued his first parliamentary speech for abolishing the wicked trade. "I trust. . . I have proved that, upon every ground, total abolition ought to take place," he told Parliament.[168] And even though backed by Burke, Pitt, and others, the issue was deferred until next session, Parliament agreeing to have the question considered under committee. Not until 1791 did the committee finish its work, yet Wilberforce was again defeated 88 to 163. Further demoralizing defeats followed in 1792 and 1793.

Then came war with France in February 1793, which had the effect of relegating the abolition of the slave trade into measure of minor importance. Though he tried a new tactic of bringing forward a bill (The Foreign Slave Bill) to prohibit the carrying of slaves to foreign shores in British ships, Wilberforce was again defeated—this time by two votes. For the next fourteen years he persevered in the fight but was repeatedly beaten: in 1796 (70 to 74), in 1797 (74 to 82), in 1798 (83 to 87), and in 1799 (54 to 84). It was not until 1804 that Wilberforce won a victory in the Commons, only to be overthrown in the House of Lords.

While continual defeats might have crushed a leader of less perseverance and determination, Wilberforce maintained a confident tenacity born of his deep religious faith. As far back as 1793 he expressed a firm determination to complete what he had begun.

> *In the case of every question of political expediency there appears to me room for consideration of times and seasons. . . But in the present instance where the actual commission of guilt is in question, a man who fears God is not at liberty. . . If I thought that the immediate Abolition of the Slave Trade would cause an insurrection in our islands, I should not for an instant remit my most serious endeavors. Be persuaded then, I shall still even less make this grand cause the sport of caprice, or sacrifice it to motives of political convenience or personal feeling.[169]*

After another defeat in 1805, a Clerk of the Commons suggested that he give up the fight. Wilberforce rebuffed him, "I do expect to carry it," he insisted, "and what is more, I feel assured that I shall carry it speedily."[170] In the face of defeat, Wilberforce smelt the scent of victory—and he was right.

The following year (1806) Parliament finally passed a bill prohibiting the "importation of slaves by British ships into Colonies annexed by Britain during the war, or into any Colonies of a foreign State, and to prohibit the outfitting of foreign slave ships in British ports, or the employment of British capital or labour therein."[171] The measure became law, and at long last the enemy was on the run.

A year later "A Bill for the Abolition of the Slave Trade" was introduced to Parliament. On February 23, 1807, abolition was secured by a vote of 287 to 16. And as the Attorney General, Sir Samuel Romilly, stood and praised the perseverance of Wilberforce, the House rose to its feet and broke out in cheers. Wilberforce was so overcome with emotion that he sat with his head in hand, tears streaming down his face.

Astonishingly, Wilberforce did not rest satisfied with his victory; for although the trade was now legally abolished, there were still men in chains. So he again took up the cause of the slaves, and again had to exercise an almost supernatural perseverance as he now pushed for the total abolition of slavery.

In spite of personal criticism, threats on his life, and deep-seated prejudice on the part of many colleagues, Wilberforce labored for an additional twenty-six years until, on July 26, 1833, the Emancipation Bill passed through Parliament.

Three days later, Wilberforce died. Perseverance had won the prize.

FRIENDSHIP

*I wish not to abate anything of the force or the frankness of your
animadversions. . . Openness is the only foundation and
preservative of friendship.*[172]

*O*ne indispensable trait of a first-class leader is his ability to develop
and maintain friendships. Whether it is called "team building" or
"networking," a leader must have the capacity to attract to himself disparate
individuals and to mold them into a committed and hard-working team.

This gift was a chief mark of Wilberforce's leadership. Indeed, without the
dedication and labor of a small group of like-minded friends, he never would
have achieved his life-long ambition of abolishing slavery in the British
Empire. As biographer Garth Lean has noted, Wilberforce needed his friends
"to make him what he was, but they needed him to transform their many
interests into a river of reform."[173] In addition to his many other talents, it was
Wilberforce's genius for friendship that enabled him to make such a profound
impact on Parliament and the nation of England. Like many other great
leaders, Wilberforce never worked alone, and from his first days in politics
he labored in tandem with a group of reformers known as "the Saints."

Chief among them was Henry Thornton, who was a close personal friend
and fellow Member of Parliament. The two had met at the home of Thornton's
father who lived in Clapham. And it was there that Wilberforce and Thornton,
in 1792, lived together as bachelors in a house purchased by Wilberforce.
Later, when each married, they stayed neighbors on the same estate in
Clapham, and "the Saints" or "Clapham Sect" began to gather around them.

Thornton was a successful banker like his father before him, and
possessed both a keen mind for abstract economics and a sound business
sense. Thus it was no surprise that when the Saints planned any of their
many social reforms they turned to Henry for practical business advice and
financial support.[174]

Granville Sharp, a brilliant and eccentric scholar, was another of
the group, and the one who originally recruited Wilberforce to the cause of

abolition. It was Sharp who, in 1772, undertook the case of a beaten and abandoned slave, and secured the famous ruling that essentially declared that any slave who set foot in English territory must be considered free. Thus, he single-handedly overturned the legal opinion of the most renowned jurists in England. Later, Sharp was the Saint who initiated the Sierra Leone project, which was designed to provide a home in Africa for any freed slaves who desired to return there.

The "chaplain" of the Clapham Sect was John Venn, the rector of the parish church in Clapham. Besides providing spiritual guidance to the group, Venn collaborated with them and led many of their causes. He started a system of parish visitation, founded the Society for Bettering the Condition of the Poor, and was the prime mover behind the national Church Missionary Society, which he founded in 1799.

Hannah More, one of the many women associated with Clapham, was a determined religious activist—so determined that it earned her the title of "petticoat bishop." A successful poet and playwright, More had hobnobbed in the fashionable intellectual circle in London, claiming David Garrick and Samuel Johnson as friends. However, after a conversion or rededication in the 1780's, More began a career as an educator and writer on behalf of the lower classes, helping to organize schools for the poor. She likewise used her pen to provide inexpensive reading material for the disadvantaged. Her *Cheap Repository Tracts,* as they were called, sold for a penny a piece, and were underwritten by Thornton. Within a year of publication, over two million were sold.[175]

Whenever Wilberforce, Thornton, or any other member of the Saints needed a fact or figure, they often quipped, "Look it up in Macaulay!"—Zachary Macaulay that is, the group's one-man research department. Indeed, Macaulay's photographic memory, tireless research, and incisive analysis made his reports so reliable that "it became a dictum that Macaulay could be quoted on the floor of the House of Commons without fear of con-tradiction."[176] After serving as governor of Sierra Leone for six years, Macaulay became, in 1802, the first editor of the *Christian Observer.* He was additionally a member of twenty-three philanthropic and religious societies, and sat on the board of nine.

The list of Wilberforce's "saints" could be expanded to include such notables as James Stephen, Charles Grant, and Thomas Clarkson—one of the most important but less appreciated of British abolitionists. But one thing is certain—despite their varied talents, their effectiveness as a team was a result of Wilberforce's ability to keep them focused on their common cause. Moreover, Wilberforce added to the group vision, and that intangible atmosphere that flowed from his optimism, charm, and friendship. Like other great leaders, the force of his own affection drew men together and mobilized their energies for a greater good.

CHARITY

A vigorous principle of enlarged and active charity springs up within us; and we go forth with alacrity, desirous of treading in the steps of our blessed Master, and of manifesting our gratitude for his unmerited goodness, by bearing each other's burdens, and abounding in the disinterested labors of benevolence.[177]

With all the political talk today about compassion and tolerance it is interesting to note that the cardinal virtue of charity means first of all love for God, and then, only secondly, love for our fellow man. Indeed, this is always the proper order. For if we presume to love men before God then we fall into the idolatry of humanism: worshipping the creature above the Creator. Yet when God has His rightful place in our minds and hearts, then we are bound—indeed, we are moved—to show genuine charity toward our neighbor. Being heavenly minded we accomplish much earthly good.

William Wilberforce was a compassionate politician because he was first and foremost a Christian statesman. After his conversion in 1784–1785, he felt that God Himself had issued him a divine call to oppose slavery and to attempt a reformation of morality in England. In both crusades he was motivated and sustained by that inner charity or love for God which was the hidden spring of all his actions, both public and private. In essence, his entire political career was the expression of his belief in the efficacy of practical Christianity.

Even while fighting the colossal struggle against slavery, Wilberforce never forgot his second great object, the "reformation of manners"—that is, his attempt to elevate the moral condition of British society. This he hoped to accomplish, first, by "suppressing vice," and secondly, by educating the upper classes on the true nature of Christianity.

Admittedly, pre-Victorian England was in need of reformation. The middle and upper classes were for the most part engrossed in splendid vices: luxurious extravagance, haughty insouciance, and rank venality. Drunkenness and adultery were common, and acceptable. As historian John Marlowe points out:

The venality of English political life was the counterpart of the coarseness and profligacy of the social life of the English governing classes. And there was a quality about it even more repellent than venality—the quality of heartlessness. There was very little to choose between the political and social morals of the English and the French aristocracy in the century before the French revolution.[178]

Furneaux succinctly summarized their moral condition, "the rich lived in a state of selfish pagan hedonism." [179]

Many in the lower classes fared little better, despite Wesley's revival, due to their brutal working conditions. Men, women, and children labored in foul, fetid factories for up to sixteen hours a day, six days a week. Women suffered and sweat in dark, dank coalmines, while their young children toiled from dawn till dusk in the colliers. Many of the poor were degraded and sottish, drowning in a sea of gin; and some destitute mothers even killed their children to sell their clothes for gin money. Law and order decayed. The government's only response was to extend the death penalty to such minor offenses as stealing a rabbit or cutting down a tree.

Wilberforce's task of reformation, therefore, was a formidable one. Yet when George III issued the traditional (but perfunctory) "Proclamation for the Encouragement of Piety and Virtue and for the Preventing of Vice, Profaneness, and Immorality," Wilberforce set to work. He established a Proclamation Society, comprised of some of Britain's most prominent leaders, designed to see that the royal proclamation became "a force rather than a farce."[180] Meanwhile, Hannah More began to write and distribute her cheap tracts to reach the lower classes with the message of morality and Christianity.

Wilberforce himself also took up his pen, and aimed it at the upper classes. In 1797, he published his *Practical View*, the aim of which is suggested by its long original title: *A Practical View of the Prevailing Religious System of Professed Christians in the Higher and Middle Classes in this Country Contrasted with Real Christianity*. His publisher, Thomas Cadell, was skeptical that a religious book by a politician would sell, and suggested that only 500 copies should be printed. Much to his surprise, the book became an instant best seller. Nearly 8,000 copies (in five editions) were sold in six months, and by 1826, it went through more editions and was translated into

French, Italian, Dutch, and German. In England, many of the upper classes read the book and were converted.

Wilberforce's crusade for the reformation of manners was not, however, merely a moral cause. He had undergone the new birth, and he desired others to experience the same enriching and ennobling experience. So, while his *Practical View* did its work on a national level, Wilberforce did his work as a fisher of men on a personal level. He took personal witnessing seriously and even kept a "Friends Paper" in his Bible. Next to the names of thirty of his friends, he jotted down ideas for how, when talking with them, he could lead casual conversations into deeper religious discussions. These "launchers," as he called them, were designed to help each of his friends take a closer step to receiving Christ. Every Sunday, Wilberforce would take his "Friends Paper" out of his Bible, review it, revise it, and pray over it.

It was Christ, more than any cause, who was at the heart of Wilberforce's crusades, and who was at the center of the Clapham Sect. They prayed together, worshipped together, supported one another, and even reproved one another in love. Each had undergone conversion, and were "pledged not only to the great causes they undertook together, but also to help their friends attain the character and destiny which God revealed for them."[181] The success of the Saints was rooted in their assurance that their sins were forgiven in Christ. "They knew," writes Roger Anstey, "not only that they could overcome evil in their own hearts but also that they could conquer the evils in the world which they felt called to combat."[182]

Understanding the true nature of charity, Wilberforce and his friends sought to love God supremely and then to serve their fellowmen sacrificially. Genuine charity, contrary to either a sentimental tolerance or indifferent pietism, was born of spiritual devotion and resulted in social action. "Faith worketh by love."[183]

Wilberforce's achievements as a reformer and philanthropist, therefore, were a product of his Christian faith and personal experience of Christ. He was not merely a humanitarian; he was a Christian. His love for God and man was the bedrock of his principled politics and compassionate crusades.

ROBERT E. LEE
(1807–1870)

Robert E. Lee was born in Stratford, Virginia, the son of Henry "Light-Horse Harry" Lee. His father, a friend of George Washington, had been a hero in the Revolutionary War and three-time governor of Virginia. When Robert was six, his father left the family for Barbados in order to regain his health and recoup his finances. He never returned. Thus, his mother, Anne Hill Carter, who was descended from one of the wealthiest families in Virginia, raised Robert alone.

Lee entered the Military Academy when he was 18, graduated second in his class in 1829, and became a lieutenant in the 1830's. In 1831 he married Mary Anne Randolph Custis, great-granddaughter of the wife of George Washington.

Lee saw military action during the Mexican War, and assisted General Winfield Scott in the capture of Vera Cruz in 1847, for which he was promoted. He was for a time the superintendent of West Point (1852–1855). When the radical abolitionist, John Brown, occupied the armory at Harper's Ferry in his attempt to incite a slave uprising, Lee was ordered to subdue Brown's force, which he easily did.

With the outbreak of the Civil War in April 1861, and Virginia's subsequent secession from the Union, Lee resigned from the federal military. He was then recruited into the Confederate Army. By summer he was given the rank of general. In June of 1862 Lee was given command of the Army of Northern Virginia, and in February, 1865, he was made general in chief of all Confederate armies.

Historians now recognize Lee as one of the greatest military strategists in history. In every battle he fought, he was always outnumbered, often two-to-one. His armies were under-fed and under-clothed, and sorely lacking in military training and supplies. Nevertheless, he achieved several major victories, and nearly won the war for the South.

Lee was deeply loved and respected by his men and even, after the war, his former enemies in the North came to appreciate his military genius, his godly character, and his gallantry and grace. He was, to friend and foe alike, a true Christian gentleman—the symbol of all that was good in the old South.

DUTY

Do your duty in all things. . . . You cannot do more; you should never do less.[184]

D uty is the one word that captures the life of Robert E. Lee. For Lee, duty meant doing the right and honorable thing. It meant fulfilling one's obligations in every area of life. It meant obedience to lawful authority, submission to hardship, and thorough completion of tasks. It meant laying aside self-interest for the benefit of others. Lee's life, according to Charles Flood, was "one long response to the call of duty."[185] Indeed it was.

Lee learned his first lessons in duty as a child. His father essentially deserted the family, his two older brothers moved from the home, and his mother was in poor health. Thus at thirteen years of age, young Robert became the head of the household. In addition to the responsibilities of school and regular chores, his duties were magnified by his mother's gradual decline into invalidism. After school he could be seen carrying her to the carriage for her daily ride, doing his best to encourage and cheer her.

As her condition worsened, the full weight of the household fell on his shoulders: he was the housekeeper, did the marketing, and looked after the horses and stables. He eventually became his mother's nurse. As one cousin recalls, Robert "mixed every dose of medicine she took, and he nursed her night and day. If Robert left the room she kept her eyes on the door till he returned. He never left her but for a short time."[186] Everyone who knew him at the time testified that he carried his cross without complaint.

Little did Lee foresee that his childhood was an adumbration of his future marriage. After the birth of his second child, Lee's wife, Mary, developed a pelvic infection that went untreated. Consequently, she increasingly suffered from severe arthritis. She lost the use of her right arm and hand, seldom slept due to pain, and by 1857 was an invalid. Despite her condition, Lee's love and devotion to her never failed. Although he was away at war, he wrote to her constantly, and also wrote to his children to watch over her and obey her. For instance, on March 1846, he wrote to one his sons:

> *You and Custis must take great care of your kind mother and*
> *dear sisters when your father is dead. To do that you must learn*
> *to be good. Be true, kind, and generous, and pray earnestly to*
> *God to enable you to "keep his commandments, and walk in the*
> *same all the days of your life."[187]*

Lee's decision to side with the South was for him equally a matter of duty. He knew that the South was unlikely to win the war. Nevertheless, he felt it a hallowed duty to stand by his native State and extended family. To turn against his home would have been the violation of a sacred trust. "If the Union is dissolved, and the Government disrupted, I shall return to my native State and share the miseries of my people, and save in defense will draw my sword on none."[188]

He did draw his sword, of course, in defense of the South. Yet after years of vigorous and valiant fighting, Lee's armies were vastly outnumbered and on the verge of starvation. Would he sacrifice their lives to enhance his reputation or would he humble himself and surrender to General Grant? As biographer Freeman rightly notes, the question for Lee in this decisive hour was a simple question of duty.

> *In his clear creed, right was duty and must be discharged. He*
> *probably never summed up this aspect of his religion more*
> *completely than in that self-revealing hour before he started to*
> *meet General Grant, when he answered all the appeals of his*
> *lieutenants with the simple statement: "The question is, is it right*
> *to surrender this army? If it's right, then I will take all the*
> *responsibility." It is a high creed—right at all times and at all*
> *costs—but daily self-discipline and a clear sense of justice made*
> *him able to adhere to it.[189]*

Years later Lee recalled his fateful decision, and characteristically framed the issue in terms of duty. "I did only what my duty demanded; I could have taken no other course without dishonor. And if all were to be done over again, I should act in precisely the same manner."[190] On another occasion, when

Pastor William Jones was bemoaning the sad defeat of the South, Lee responded, "Yes, all that is very sad, and might be a cause of self-reproach, but that we are conscious that we have humbly tried to do our duty."[191]

After the war, Lee was already a military legend and was offered many profitable posts. For instance, an insurance company offered him $10,000 a year just to use his name; and another firm proffered him a salary of $50,000 (a fortune in those days). Lee declined them both. Instead he responded to the call of duty. He took the position of president of a small, bankrupt college in the South. "I have a self-imposed task which I must accomplish," he said. "I have led the young men of the South in battle; I have seen many of them die on the field; I shall devote my remaining energies to training young men to do their duty in life."[192]

One of Lee's favorite maxims was, "You cannot be a true man until you learn to obey."[193] And during his tenure as president of Washington College (later renamed Washington and Lee College), he strove to inculcate in the students his own code of conduct. When asked about the school's rules of behavior, Lee replied, "We have but one rule here, and it is that every student must be a gentleman."[194] For Lee this meant diligence, honorable conduct, faithful worship, and respect for authority. In other words, do your duty at work, do your duty toward others, and do your duty before God.

There is no better credo for today's leaders than the one Lee once wrote to himself:

There is a true glory and a true honor: the glory of duty done—the honor of the integrity of principle.[195]

DISCIPLINE

*I cannot consent to place in the control of others one
who cannot control himself.*[196]

H istory is strewn with the tragic figures of great and gallant men who fell victim to their own passions. Gifts and talents notwithstanding, their lack of personal discipline led to a dreadful downfall.

Robert E. Lee's own father is a doleful example of this truth. Of noble lineage and graced with courage and patriotism, Henry Lee was one the Virginia's finest Revolutionary War heroes. He served with distinction under Washington, and after the war his oratory and popularity propelled him into the governor's mansion for three terms. Henry, however, had a fondness for land speculation; and as a result he financially ruined himself. Historian Douglas Freeman notes, "For the chief weakness of his character now showed itself in a wild mania for speculation. His every scheme was grandiose, and his profits ran to millions in his mind. He plunged deeply, and always unprofitably."[197]

By 1809, when Robert was only sixteen months old, his father, in a final attempt to pay off his debts, had to deed away nearly all his property. He was stripped bare; yet his obligations were not met. In April of 1809 Henry was arrested for a debt of 5,400 Spanish dollars and confined to jail. Not long after his release the following spring, Henry got involved in an anti-war protest and was sorely beaten and disfigured. For all intents, he was now a broken man. "Hope was dead now in the heart of Henry Lee."[198] Disgraced and disfigured, Henry "Light Horse Harry" Lee—onetime hero and statesman—left his beloved country and family in the summer of 1813, never to return. The warrior-patriot became a wandering pauper.

In stark contrast to his father, and perhaps due to his admonitory example, Robert became a model of self-control and self-discipline. Indeed, his father's financial failures required his family to exercise frugal management in the home. His mother, both out of monetary necessity and maternal sympathy, trained young Robert and her other children not to emulate their father's penchant for indulgence. "Self-denial, self-control, and the strictest economy in all financial matters were part of the code of honor she taught them from infancy. These qualities were inculcated in Robert so deeply that they became fundamentals of his character."[199]

Lee's rigorous training paid off in his military career. His courage, which is really fear under control, was obvious. During the Mexican War, for example, General Scott said that Lee demonstrated "the greatest feat of physical and moral courage performed by any individual."[200] And throughout the War Between the States, Lee was frequently at the front lines and had to be forced to the rear by his own troops who would not charge while he was in danger. Shouts of "Go back, General Lee!" and "Lee to the back!" were often heard during the heat of battle.

Lee also displayed his discipline by sharing in the physical needs of his men. His troops were usually lacking in food, and Lee would not indulge himself while his men suffered. Although he was fond of fine foods, during the war he maintained a lean diet and shared his meager meals with others. Whenever luxuries were sent to him because he was a General, he usually either sent it to a hospital or gave it to his troops. His typical lunch was boiled cabbage in salt water. During the evacuation of Petersburg, General Ewell visited Lee's headquarters during dinner. Unable to stay, Lee insisted that Ewell take his dinner, which consisted of two small, cold sweet potatoes, one of Lee's favorite foods.

Lee's self-denial shines through the following account given by historian Steven Wilkins.

During the siege of Petersburg, at a special Christmas dinner to which he had been invited, he was embarrassed that the hostess discovered him not eating his portion of turkey. When asked about it, he said he wanted to save his portion so that he could carry it to one of his staff officers who had been very ill and had eaten nothing "but corn bread and sweet-potato coffee."[201]

Later, much to Lee's surprise, his generous host in Petersburg sent a barrel of turkeys to the camp—one for each officer. Though grateful for the gift, Lee ordered his turkey sent to the hospital. His example of self-denial rebuked the other officers and they "sadly repacked the barrel" and sent all its contents to the hospital.[202]

Some of the severest tests of Lee's self-control came after the war. He could have easily become a wealthy man just by allowing a New York insurance agency to use his prestigious name: they offered him one million dollars to make him president with no obligations. His father's dream of easy money! Yet Lee refused. He chose rather to serve an obscure, dilapidated college that could only afford to pay him a small salary.

Perhaps most significantly of all, Lee refused to succumb to bitterness after his defeat and surrender. His nobility in defeat, for which he was much praised, was partly a reflection of his self-control. While others, including his own wife, were vehement in their denunciation of the Federal tyranny, Lee mastered his emotions and realized that public accusations would only stir up hatred. He repeatedly advised reconciliation for the good of the country. Once, while visiting White Sulpher Springs, a young woman asked Lee if he felt resentment toward his former enemies. "I believe I may say looking into my own heart, and speaking as in the presence of God," he gravely responded, "that I have never known one moment of bitterness or resentment." He then admonished her to tell her friends that "it is unworthy of them as women, and especially as Christian women, to cherish feelings of resentment against the North."[203]

Lee was not austere; he was simply disciplined. He knew from his father's fate that unless a man learns to govern himself he is unfit to govern others, and may land himself in ruin. Discipline, which means exercising self-control and self-denial, is foundational to a leader's success. That was the lesson Lee strove to teach by word and example.

Shortly before his death, a young mother brought her baby to Lee for a blessing. As the white-haired General lifted the child in his arms, he gazed at the infant and pondered. Then, turning to the mother, he deliberately uttered the message of his own life, "Teach him he must deny himself."[204]

SPIRITUALITY

Above all things, learn at once to worship your Creator and to do His will as revealed in His Holy Book.[205]

H aving studied the life of Lee for over ten years, historian Douglas Southall Freeman judiciously identified the invisible fountain of his personal greatness. "Robert Lee was one of the small company of great men in whom there is no inconsistency to be explained, no enigma to be solved. What he seemed, he was—a wholly human gentleman, the essential elements of whose positive character were two and only two, simplicity and spirituality."[206] Freeman then went on to explain that Lee's "spirituality" was in fact the Christian faith.

To understand the faith of Robert E. Lee is to fill out the picture of him as a gentleman of simple soul. For him religion blended with the code of nobless oblige to which he had been reared. Together, these two forces resolved every problem of his life into right and wrong. There cannot be said to have been a "secret" of his life, but this assuredly was the great, transparent truth, and this it was, primarily, that gave to his career its consistency and decision. Over his movements as a soldier he hesitated often, but over his acts as a man, never. There was but one question ever: What was his duty as a Christian and a gentleman? That he answered by the sure criterion of right and wrong, and, having answered, acted. Everywhere the two obligations went together; he never sought to expiate as a Christian for what he had failed to do as a gentleman, or to atone as a gentleman for what he had neglected as a Christian. He could not have conceived of a Christian who was not a gentleman.[207]

Not surprisingly Lee's first lessons in piety came from his mother. She had him baptized in the Episcopal Church and drilled him in the catechism. As a child he attended Christ Church in Alexandra, and under the preaching of Reverend William Meade was grounded in the fundamentals of evangelical Protestantism: original sin, the necessity of faith and conversion, the inerrancy of the Scriptures, the deity of Christ, and the providence of God.[208]

Lee never departed from his childhood faith and throughout his life regularly attended public worship. Even during the war Lee attended public worship and encouraged his troops to do likewise. To this end he issued a general order (#15, dated 7 February 1864) requiring that "none but duties strictly necessary shall be required to be performed on Sunday" so that his men could give their attention to "religious exercises."[209] When revival broke out amongst the Confederate armies, Lee made it a habit to encourage the chaplains in their evangelistic work, and to attend the preaching of the Word. Once, a war correspondent from Richmond visited the camp and accompanied Lee to a service. He later reported that in response to the preaching of Pastor Benjamin Lacey, Lee was moved to tears.[210]

When Reverend Lacey once reported to Lee that the chaplains and troops were concerned for him and prayed for him, Lee responded, "I sincerely thank you for that, and I can only say that I am a poor sinner, trusting in Christ alone for salvation and that I need all the prayers you can offer for me."[211]

Of course, it is not uncommon for public men to make public professions. Yet Lee's faith was real, as evidenced by his strict observance of private and family devotions. Every day began with private prayer. "No day should be lived unless it was begun with a prayer of thankfulness and an intercession for guidance," he once said.[212] Afterward, he presided over family prayers. The day then ended as it began. The household would gather and Lee would read Scripture to his family and guide them in prayer.

Lee's private and public devotions were grounded in the Bible, which he held to be the inspired Word of God. "There are many things in the old Book which I may never be able to explain," he once said, "but I accept it as the infallible Word of God, and receive its teachings as inspired by the Holy Ghost."[213] Through the Bible, Lee found comfort, wisdom, and salvation. "I prefer the Bible to any other book," he confessed. "There is enough in that to satisfy the most ardent thirst for knowledge; to open the way to true wisdom; and to teach the only road to salvation and eternal happiness."[214]

Lee wished to share the blessings of the Bible with others, and his reverence and confidence in the Bible was manifested by his distribution of the Scriptures. During the war he had the Bible distributed to his troops, and some time later he accepted the post of president of the Rockbridge County Bible Society, a post he held to his death. He served in that position, he said, because he was zealous to cooperate "in any way I can in extending the inestimable knowledge of the priceless truths of the Bible."[215]

Lee's faith in God and His Word was a far cry from today's easy-believism. Sorely tested by bloody war and bitter defeat, he maintained a steadfast faith in God's good providence. In victory he gave "all the glory to the Lord of host, from whom all glories are;" and in defeat he admonished his men, "Soldiers! We have sinned against Almighty God."[216]

When the final defeat came, Lee accepted the outcome without bitterness because he trusted in God's ability to work all things together for good. Writing to an old friend, George W. Jones, he professed, "We failed, we failed, but in the good providence of God apparent failure often proves a blessing."[217] Freeman has correctly observed that Lee's courage in war and nobility in defeat can only be understood when we realize that "he submitted himself in all things faithfully to the will of a Divinity which, in his simple faith, was directing wisely the fate of nations and the daily life of His children."[218]

The greatness of Lee, then, is directly attributable to his Christian faith and practice. He was a Christian gentleman whose noble character and virtue reflected his devotion to God. Author Benjamin Howell Griswold, in *The Spirit of Lee and Jackson,* has rightly perceived this connection.

Lee and Jackson were both professing Christians—most men of their day were that—but on the premise that these men not only professed Christianity, but actually practiced it and endeavored in every way to live according to its much neglected tenets. They were great readers of the Bible, and nearly every act of their lives was directed by their interpretation of its maxims. This was true of their action not only at home toward their family and neighbors, but even in the camp and on the battlefield toward their enemies . . . Humility, Purity, Peacemaking, Love of Righteousness—

Righteousness—virtues neglected—if not a little despised today, seem to have exalted these men and lifted them from the depths of defeat to the pinnacle of fame.[219]

Truly they did. For the virtue that springs from faith is the only sure key to greatness and fame.

BOOKER T. WASHINGTON
(1856–1915)

Booker T. Washington, well known as the founder of the famed Tuskegee Institute in Alabama, was an educational reformer and leader of the black race in America during the era of segregation. Born a slave in Franklin County, Virginia, Washington gained his freedom as a result of the Emancipation Proclamation, and shortly thereafter his family moved to Malden, West Virginia, five miles from Charleston.

From 1865 to 1871 Washington worked in the local coal and salt mines and also served as a houseboy for a local mine owner. Always eager of gaining an education, however, Washington enrolled in Hampton Normal and Agricultural Institute in the fall of 1872, then under the direction of General Samuel C. Armstrong. After successfully graduating, Washington returned to Malden as a schoolteacher and social worker.

In 1881 Washington was called to become the founding principal of a new normal school for black students at Tuskegee. There Washington labored to reproduce the Hampton model of thrift, hard work, and virtuous living. The primary aim of Tuskegee was to teach young Afro-Americans the dignity of labor and a practical skill as the means to self-improvement.

In addition to his work at Tuskegee, Washington started many forms of rural extension work, established the National Negro Business League, the National Negro Health Week, and various other conferences. Washington also wrote numerous articles and books that articulated his vision for black education and self-improvement. His autobiographical Up From Slavery *is a minor classic and is still widely read.*

It was not until 1893, however, when Washington spoke at the Cotton States and International Exposition at Atlanta (the Atlanta Exposition), that Washington became a national figure. In response to his brief but powerful address, he was almost instantly recognized as the successor of Frederick Douglas, who had just died, as leader of the black race in America.

WORK

*Nothing ever comes to one, that is worth having, except as a
result of hard work.*[220]

P erhaps one of the strongest delusions regarding leadership is the notion
that leaders are accorded privileges and perks while simultaneously
being exempted from work. Lazy leadership is, in fact, an oxymoron. And any
man who aspires to leadership for the sake of ease is in for a rude awakening.
The harsh reality is that the path to success is strewn with thorns not
roses; and once a man achieves any amount of substantial attainment he must
continue a rigorous work schedule in order to maintain the benefit of
his accomplishments.

Even success itself must be gauged by the amount of work one expends
in clearing his path of obstacles. As Washington himself put it, "I have
learned that success is to be measured not so much by the position that one
has reached in life as by the obstacles which he has overcome while trying
to succeed."[221]

If there is one word that sums up the secret of Booker T. Washington's rise
from indigent slavery to national fame and success as a leader, it is that small
and often despised word—work. For Washington, work was both a personal
way of life and a public philosophy of race improvement.

From his earliest days as a slave, Washington became accustomed to
demanding physical labor. "From the time that I can remember anything," he
recounted later in life, "almost every day of my life has been occupied in some
kind of labor."[222] When his mother Jane moved the family to Malden,
Washington's stepfather put him to work in the mines. "Though I was a mere
child, my stepfather put me and my brother at work in one of the furnaces.
Often I began work as early as four o'clock in the morning."[223]

Washington never expressed bitterness at having to work as a child except
that it interfered with his desire to get an education. In fact, when an elemen-
tary school for black children was opened in Malden, Washington worked five
hours *before* school, and then returned to the mines in the afternoon. Some

time later he went to work as houseboy of Mrs. Ruffner, where he worked all day and continued his education at night. And it was she who taught Washington the importance of doing his work in a prompt and systematic manner.

On his first day at Hampton in 1872, Washington learned the tangible reward of hard work. Having traveled for days without proper boarding or a change of clothes, he presented himself to the head teacher looking like " a worthless loafer or tramp." Not knowing whether to admit or refuse him, the head teacher made Washington wait while she admitted other students. After several hours had passed, she said to him, "The adjoining recitation-room needs sweeping. Take the broom and sweep it."[224] Washington tackled the job with enthusiasm.

> *I swept the recitation-room three times. Then I got a dusting-cloth and I dusted it four times. All the woodwork around the wall, every bench, table, and desk, I went over four times with my dusting-cloth. Besides, every piece of furniture had been moved and every closet and corner in the room had been thoroughly cleaned. I had the feeling that in large measure my future depended upon the impression I made upon the teacher in the cleaning of that room. When I was through, I reported to the head teacher. She was a "Yankee" woman who knew just where to look for dirt. She went into the room and inspected the floor and closets; then she took her handkerchief and rubbed it on the woodwork about the walls, and over the table and benches. When she was unable to find one bit of dirt on the floor, or a particle of dust on any of the furniture, she quietly remarked, "I guess you will do to enter this institution."[225]*

Sweeping that room was Washington's entrance exam, and he passed it with flying colors. In fact, it paved the way for his entire stay at Hampton. He did such a good job cleaning the recitation-room that he was offered the position of school janitor, which provided him the income to pay his tuition. "The work was hard and taxing, but I stuck to it," Washington later recalled. "I had a large number of rooms to care for, and had to work late into the night, while at the same time I had to rise by four o'clock in the morning, in order to build the fires and have a little time in which to prepare my lessons."[226]

Washington's entire career at Hampton was one long lesson on the importance of hard work. Many years later he noted in his autobiography, *Up From Slavery*,

> *At Hampton I not only learned that it was not a disgrace to labour, but learned to love labour, not alone for its financial value, but for labour's own sake and for the independence and self-reliance which the ability to do something which the world wants done brings. At that institution I got my first taste of what it meant to live a life of unselfishness, my first knowledge of the fact that the happiest individuals are those who do the most to make others useful and happy.[227]*

After leaving Hampton, Washington exemplified and proudly proclaimed the gospel of work. He returned to Malden for a few years as a teacher, regularly working fourteen hours a day, seven days a week. When, in 1881, he was called to undertake the establishment of Tuskegee, he consciously sought to replicate his experience at Hampton by teaching the students the honor and dignity of work, even the kind of physical work that many had come to associate with slavery.

Throughout his tenure as the principal of Tuskegee, Washington insisted that the students themselves build the institution. They cleared the land, chopped the wood, raised the crops and animals to sell at fund-raisers, prepared their own meals, made their own bricks, and constructed their own classrooms, dormitories, and administrative buildings. The subsequent growth of the school was living proof of the efficacy of Washington's gospel of labor. Beginning his school with neither land nor building, the first classes were held in a dilapidated shanty. Yet by the time of Washington's death, Tuskegee was an impressive educational institution with more than one hundred buildings, over two thousand acres of land, an endowment of $2,000,000 and an annual budget of nearly $300,000. The nearly two hundred instructors taught over fifteen hundred students in thirty-eight trades and professions.[228]

The success of Tuskegee, as well as the success of Washington himself, was the simple outgrowth of his doctrine of thrift and the dignity of labor. This doctrine permeated many of his public addresses, especially the Atlanta Exposition speech that made him famous.

> *Our greatest danger is that in the great leap from slavery to freedom we may overlook the fact that the masses of us are to live by the productions of our hands, and fail to keep in mind that we shall prosper in proportion as we learn to dignify and glorify common labor and put brains and skill in to the common occupations of life; shall prosper in proportion as we learn to draw the line between the superficial and the substantial, the ornamental gew-gaws of life and the useful. No race can prosper till it learns that there is as much dignity in tilling a field as in writing a poem. It is at the bottom of life we must begin, and not at the top.*[229]

Real prosperity and progress will always be the result of hard work. Natural gifts alone will never carry the day. A true leader knows this, and does not seek the easy life but the strenuous life.[230] While others play he will work; while others hug the pillow he will burn the candle. "The price of success," Washington once told the National Negro Business League, "means beginning at the bottom; it means struggle, it means hardship, it often means hunger, it means planning and sacrificing today that you may possess and enjoy tomorrow; and if you sit idly by and let the other fellow think and plan and lie awake at night, you can rest assured that the other fellow is going to control business everywhere. . ."[231]

Like Washington, a leader will not seek privileges but opportunities— opportunities to labor for the good of himself and others. In that way the dignity of his labor will lend dignity to his leadership.

OPTIMISM

No one likes to feel that he is continually following a funeral procession.[232]

*L*abor without hope is drudgery. To work day and night at seemingly trivial tasks without a vision for victory is to be caught in a cycle of despair. Therefore, one of the greatest challenges of leadership is to inspire people to believe that they can overcome apparently insurmountable obstacles, and that in the end, their labor will not be in vain. Simply put, a leader must be able to inspire hope.

When the Civil War ended, blacks in the South emerged from their shackles without education, skill, land, or capital and were thus unable to seize the opportunities of their newfound freedom. In addition to the impediments of poverty and ignorance, they continually lived under the shadow of the white hood. During the post-reconstruction era, racial discrimination, segregation, unjust oppression, denial of suffrage and other civil rights, and even the threat of lynching haunted post-bellum blacks.

In spite of these disadvantages and inequalities, Washington refused to dwell on his people's hardships. Instead, he was eternally optimistic and constantly stressed the blessings of adversity. Whining about problems was not the way to achieve success, either as an individual or as a race. Washington accepted that life was hard, and believed the best approach was to be positive and constructive rather than always emphasizing grievances.

Even though the injuries to blacks were very real, Washington insisted on seeing the positive side of the racial situation. For instance, in 1912 he noted in a newspaper article that there had been seventy-one cases of lynching in the past year, yet he still contended that blacks in America were better situated than blacks elsewhere in the world.

Despite all any one has said or can say in regard to the injustice and unfair treatment of the people of my race at the hands of the white men in this country, I venture to say that there is no example in history of the people of one race who have had the assistance, the direction, and the sympathy of another race in all its efforts to rise to such an extent as the Negro in the United States. Notwithstanding all the defects in our system of dealing with him, the Negro in this country owns more property, lives in better houses, is in a larger measure encouraged in business, eats better food, has more schoolhouses and churches, more teachers and ministers than any similar group of Negroes anywhere else in the world.[233]

As the newly recognized leader of the black race, Washington knew that it fell to him to convince his people that prejudicial barriers to progress could be removed by patient and persistent effort. Therefore, his educational goals at Tuskegee were more than merely utilitarian. His goal was to inspire hope by providing tools for self-improvement. "From the very outset of my work," he wrote, "it has been my steadfast purpose to establish an institution that would provide instruction, not for the select few, but for the masses, giving them standards and ideals, and inspiring in them hope and courage to go patiently forward."[234]

How could Washington be so optimistic when faced with hardship, prejudice, and even physical violence? First of all, like all great leaders he insisted on seeing opportunities where others saw only obstacles; he was determined to see possibilities when others saw only problems. It was true that Afro-Americans were being mistreated by many whites, yet Washington believed that complaining was counter-productive. In spite of the many prejudices and problems, there lay before the black race a wealth of opportunities to be seized by hopeful determination. When he addressed the National Colored Teachers Association in St. Louis in 1911, Washington challenged black teachers to inculcate a hopeful attitude in their students.

We should see to it too that we not only emphasize in our work as teachers the opportunities that are before our race, but should also emphasize the fact that we ought to become a hopeful, encouraged race. There is no hope for any man or woman, whatever his color, who is pessimistic; who is continually whining and crying about his condition. There is hope for any people, however handicapped by difficulties, that makes up its mind that it will succeed, that it will make success the stepping stone to a life of success and usefulness.[235]

Secondly, Washington maintained and inspired hope because he believed hard work would inevitably lead to progress. When he himself was awarded an honorary degree of Master of Arts from Harvard University in 1896, Washington told the Harvard Alumni:

If through me, a humble representative, seven million of my people in the South might be permitted to send a message to Harvard—Harvard that offered up on death's altar, young Shaw, and Russell, and Lowell, and scores of others, that we might have a free and united country—that message would be, "Tell them that the sacrifice was not in vain. Tell them that by the way of the shop, the field, the skilled hand, habits of thrift and economy, by way of industrial school and college, we are coming. We are crawling up, working up, yea, bursting up. Often through oppression, unjust discrimination, and prejudice, but through them we are coming up, and with proper habits, intelligence, and property, there is no power on earth that can permanently stay our progress."[236]

Thirdly, Washington expected that, eventually and inevitably, genuine accomplishment and talent—what he called "merit"—could not be forever ignored or suppressed. "Say what we will, there is something in human nature which we cannot blot out, which makes one man, in the end, recognize and reward merit in another, regardless of colour or race." In the closing chapter of his optimistic and inspiring autobiography, *Up From Slavery*, Washington reiterated his confidence that merit must triumph.

> *Despite superficial and temporary signs which might lead one to entertain a contrary opinion, there was never a time when I felt more hopeful for the race than I do at the present. The great human law that in the end recognizes and rewards merit is everlasting and universal.*[237]

Finally, Washington was optimistic because he embraced the Christian worldview. Speaking before the Afro-American Council in Louisville in 1903, he reminded them of the Christian view of adversity.

> *And not the least of the blessings of such struggle is that it keeps one humble and nearer to the heart of the Giver of all gifts. Show me the individual who is permitted to go through life without anxious thought, without ever having experienced a sense of poverty and wrong, want and struggle, and I will show you a man who is likely to fail in life. "Whom the Lord loveth, He chasteneth. . ."*[238]

When Washington spoke these words, most blacks in America were consigned to the lowest forms of labor, segregated from whites, and stripped of political power. Their legal emancipation was a mockery, if not a fiction. Yet in spite of these painful and tragic obstacles an entire generation of Afro-Americans was given, despite their present miserable lot, an alternative to despair—the faith that someday their dogged and diligent efforts would be crowned with success.

In a word, Washington gave them hope. This was perhaps one of his greatest achievements, and also one of the indispensable marks of a great leader.

REALISM

An ounce of application is worth a ton of abstraction.[239]

Although it might sound contradictory, Washington's optimism was based on a solid realism. Instead of being a mere visionary with grandiose dreams and no practical means, Washington was always a leader who demanded to know actual facts and conditions rather than be enamored with attractive abstractions. He understood that the first job of a leader is to define reality.

Washington's realism is clearly evident in his whole approach to education. For the most part he believed that education must be practical or utilitarian. Not that he despised the liberal arts; but in light of the current realities facing blacks in the post-reconstruction era, he believed that progress could only be made by a steady growth in learning useful trades that in turn would improve the economic condition of Afro-Americans. If blacks were to be accepted by the white majority they must first prove that they could be industrious and useful artisans and farmers who contributed to the economic well-being of the entire community.

As one author has noted, Washington's educational philosophy was designed to convince the white majority that blacks were fitted for their freedom.

Washington was convinced that the Negro must prove himself, must demonstrate tangibly and concretely that he was worthy of the blessings of liberty. He must destroy the stereotype which years of slavery had fixed in the minds of even his friends and eliminate each of the negative slave characteristics which still clung to him. He must substitute efficiency for the slipshod work of slavery days, responsibility for irresponsibility, knowledge for ignorance and superstition, accepted moral standards for the amorality of the slave quarters. The blame for the Negro's

shortcomings was academic; the shortcomings were real and
had to be remedied.[240]

To this end, all the instruction at Tuskegee was intensely practical, a welding of theory and practice. For instance, in mathematics class, male students would have to calculate numbers of bricks to build a structure or the length of a board to finish a carpentry project; while the girls might be required to compute the number of yards of cloth needed to make dresses of various sizes. And, of course, the students themselves, as part of their practical education, did all of the work at the school.

In spite of the obvious success of Tuskegee and other projects headed by Washington, both his educational scheme and his optimistic philosophy were vehemently attacked by a small group of black critics who believed that he was consigning blacks to informal servitude through manual labor, and that Washington was naive about black prospects for the future. These critics were, by and large, a group of black intellectuals who differed temperamentally and experientially from Washington. The most notable of them, for example, was W.E.B. Du Bois, who was born in Massachusetts, educated in the public schools, and did not experience discrimination until he visited the South as an adult. Moreover, Du Bois was an "intellectual" who had studied in Europe, earned a graduate degree from Harvard, and was a college professor. He claimed that Washington's gospel of work was unnecessarily narrow and overshadowed the "higher aims of life," by which he meant the life of the mind or intellectual pursuits.

In response to the criticisms of Du Bois and others, Washington did not disclaim the value of the liberal arts, yet he maintained that the actual needs of black people in the South demanded a utilitarian education. "I have gotten a large part of my education from actual contact with things, rather than through the medium of books," he once said. "I like to deal with things as far as possible at firsthand in the way that the carpenter deals with wood, the blacksmith with iron, and the farmer with the earth." The problem with his "intellectual" critics, he asserted, was that they "understand theories but they do not understand things. . . They know books but they do not know men. They know a great deal about the slavery controversy, for example, but they know almost nothing about the Negro. Especially are they ignorant in regard to the actual needs of the masses of colored people in the South today."[241]

This was not mere cant. Washington made it his business when he arrived at Tuskegee to actually visit people in the community and observe how they lived. As he relates in his autobiography:

> I reached Tuskegee, as I have said, early in June, 1881. The first month I spent in finding accommodations for the school, and in travelling through Alabama, examining into the actual life of the people in the country districts, and in getting the school advertised among the class of people that I wanted to have attend it. The most of my travelling was done over the country roads, with a mule and a carat of a mule and a buggy wagon for conveyance. I ate and slept with the people, in their little cabins. I saw their farms, their schools, their churches. Since, in the case of the most of these visits, there had been no notice given in advance that a stranger was expected, I had the advantage of seeing the real, everyday life of the people.[242]

What did Washington observe during these impromptu visits? Usually he found that the family lived and slept in one room; that there was seldom any provision for washing or bathing within the house; that the common diet was pork fat and corn bread—the pottage of slaves; and that most families had never learned the practice of a common meal or common etiquette.

What irked Washington most was when he observed that a poor family living in a single-room cabin without the bare necessities of life would spend its money on expensive but useless or unused items. In one instance, he sat down to dinner with a family of four and noticed that there was only one fork for all of them to use; yet in the corner of the cabin was an expensive organ for which the family was spending sixty dollars in monthly installments. "One fork, and a sixty-dollar organ!" exclaimed Washington. He was incredulous.[243]

Washington's realism can be seen in his approach to the problem of racism. While his critics claimed that he was training blacks for servitude and that he should be more vocal in his opposition to discrimination, Washington recognized that the success of Tuskegee in particular, and the black race in general, was dependent on three groups: the "best class" of Southerners, philanthropic Northerners, and the majority of blacks. It is not surprising that Washington's philosophy of thrift, hard work, and virtuous living was fitted to appeal to each of these three groups. To those with the power and money to help disadvantaged blacks, Washington promised a salve to their conscience and the economic incentive that would result from a well-trained but orderly work force. To the blacks, Washington offered an obtainable and useful means for self-improvement and the inspiration that comes from hope.

Although he did protest injustice, Washington realized that bitter denunciation would only alienate the white majority and would not improve the conditions of the black minority. His view, he once said, was that blacks "needed a policy, not of destruction, but of construction; not of defense, but of aggression; a policy, not of hostility or surrender, but of friendship and advance."[244]

Washington's speech to the Afro-American Council in 1903 epitomizes his advocacy of work, his optimistic outlook, and his realistic approach to the problems confronting his race.

> *In our efforts to go forward. . . we should bear in mind that our ability and our progress will be measured largely by evidences of tangible, visible worth. We have a right in a conservative and sensible manner to enter our complaints, but we shall make a fatal error if we yield to the temptation of believing that mere opposition to our wrongs, and the simple utterance of complaint, will take the place of progressive, constructive action, which must constitute the bedrock of all true civilization. The weakest race or individual can condemn a policy; it is the work of a statesman to construct one. A race is not measured by its ability to condemn, but to create. Let us hold up our heads and with firm and steady tread go manfully forward.*[245]

Sound advice, not only for a beleaguered people, but also for any aspiring leader.

THEODORE ROOSEVELT

(1858–1919)

Theodore Roosevelt was born at home in New York City, the second of four children. After a sickly childhood in which he spent much time studying nature and reading books, Roosevelt entered Harvard College in 1876. Four months after graduation, he married Alice Lee in 1880.

After attending Columbia University Law School, Roosevelt entered politics as a New York state legislator (1881). Upon the untimely death of his wife Alice, he explored the Dakota Territory for solace, leading the life of a cowboy and author. He returned to politics in 1886 and subsequently served as Civil Service Commissioner, New York City Police Commissioner, and Assistant Secretary of the Navy under William McKinley.

With the outbreak of the Spanish-American War, Roosevelt organized the First Volunteer Cavalry Regiment (the Rough Riders) and was commissioned as a lieutenant colonel. His successful charge up San Juan Hill made Roosevelt a national hero—and a political asset. Thereafter he was elected as governor of New York (1899) and was chosen as vice president to McKinley in the election of 1900. On September 6, 1901, an assassin mortally wounded President McKinley, who died eight days later. At the age of forty-two Roosevelt became the youngest president in the history of the United States. He was returned to the White House again in 1904 by a landslide victory and awarded the Nobel Peace Prize in 1905.

*Roosevelt was simultaneously a successful writer. He penned several biographies (*Thomas Hart Benton, Gouverneur Morris, *and* Oliver Cromwell*); political manifestoes (*Essays on Practical Politics, American Ideals, Progressive Principles, Social Justice, *and* Popular Rule*); and helped create the genre of the wild west (*Hunting Trips of a Ranchman, The Winning of the West, *and* Trail and Campfire*).*

Throughout his political career, Roosevelt was known as a reformer who fought corruption, privilege, and unjust profiteering. His political crusades focused on the need for representative government, equality of opportunity, and safe working conditions for laborers. Sometimes progressive and sometimes conservative, Roosevelt consistently pursued the goal of personal morality and civic righteousness.

ACTION

There is not room in our healthy American life for the mere idler, for the man or the woman whose object it is throughout life to shirk the duties which life ought to bring. Life can mean nothing worth meaning, unless its prime aim is the doing of duty, the achievement of results worth achieving.[246]

*T*heodore Roosevelt was one of those rare individuals who combined intellectual brilliancy, athletic prowess, personal productivity, and political achievement. He wrote and preached what he called "the strenuous life," but more importantly he lived it. He was first and foremost a man of action.

By the time he was fifty, he had served as a state legislator, the under secretary of the Navy, police commissioner, U.S. civil service commissioner, New York governor, U.S. vice president, and president. Furthermore, he ran a cattle ranch in the Dakotas, worked as a journalist for several journals and newspapers, read voraciously, and composed over forty books himself. As if he had time to spare, Roosevelt also was a devoted family man, a Sunday School teacher, and an amateur hunter, boxer, taxidermist, botanist, and ornithologist.

Roosevelt's zest for life was both captivating and fatiguing. His energy seemed inexhaustible. Henry Cabot Lodge called him "a living tornado." Henry Adams noted that Roosevelt "crams more into a day than most men can hope to in a month." Some people got tired watching him work. John Hay, for instance, once quipped, "I get tired just thinking about his schedule."[247]

On one occasion Roosevelt's good friend, Jacob Riis, visited the governor's mansion and found him getting a shave and haircut. While in the barber's chair he cradled a lap desk for reviewing his mail, and simultaneously dictated to the three secretaries hovering around him. To one, he was dictating his biography on Cromwell; to another, outlining legislative objectives; and to the third, drafting an upcoming speech. Riis was astounded, yet Roosevelt said he was just trying "to make the most of the time."[248]

Roosevelt played as hard as he worked. He loved the outdoors and would hike, hunt, or fish every chance he got. Even while President he would often lead visiting dignitaries on hikes through Rock Creek Park. He also loved sailing, swimming, riding, and climbing. Once, while President, as he was climbing in the Adirondacks, he had a Secret Service agent lower him over a gorge with a rope tied round his ankles so he could photograph a bird's nest. Unable to retrieve the President, Roosevelt told the agent to "cut the rope." Fearing that the President might be harmed by the thirty-foot fall into the rushing water below, he refused. After an argument, Roosevelt ended the stalemate by cutting the rope himself. By the time the agent had scaled the rocks to the bottom, Roosevelt was lying on the water's edge, cut, bruised, and drenched. Looking up at the agent, the dazed President smiled and said, "My, wasn't that just bully!"[249]

Roosevelt matched his physical activity with mental curiosity. He was hungry for knowledge and read at least five books a week. Accordingly, he was one of the most learned men of his day, and probably the most educated man ever to capture the U.S. presidency. English diplomat Lord Charnwood asserted of Roosevelt, "No statesman for centuries has had his width of intellectual range."[250] According to Viscount Lee, "Whether the subject of the moment was political economy, the Greek drama, tropical fauna or flora, the Irish sagas, protective coloration in nature, metaphysics, the technique of football, or post-futurist painting, he was equally at home with the experts and drew out the best that was in them."[251]

If alive today, Roosevelt would probably be tagged as a neurotic workaholic. Yet his irrepressible energy resulted from his philosophy of life— what he called "the strenuous life." Due to a sickly childhood, he had to "make his body" as well as his mind. And ever since his younger days in the gym and boxing ring, Roosevelt espoused the philosophy of "bodily vigor as a method of getting that vigor of soul without which vigor of the body counts for nothing."[252]

Simply put, vigorous application is the key to success.

> *There are two kinds of success, or rather two kinds of ability*
> *displayed in the achievement of success. There is, first, the success*
> *either in big things or small things which comes to the man who*

has in him the natural power to do what no one else can do, and
what no amount of training, no perseverance or will power, will
enable any ordinary man to do. . . But much the commoner type
of success in every walk of life and in every species of effort is
that which comes to the man who differs from his fellows not
by the kind of quality which he possesses but by the degree of
development which he has given that quality.[253]

Roosevelt believed that his own achievements were merely the product of "hard labor and the exercise of my best judgment and careful planning and working long in advance."[254] He thought that the average man could, like himself, achieve greatness by dynamic endeavor.

I wish to preach, not the doctrine of ignoble ease, but the doctrine
of the strenuous life; the life of toil and effort; of labor and strife;
to preach that highest form of success which comes, not to the man
who desires more easy peace, but to the man who does not shrink
from danger, from hardship or from bitter toil, and who out of
these wins the splendid ultimate triumph.[255]

And what was true of the individual was also true of America as a nation. Roosevelt believed that her greatness was a product of effort and valor. "America has not attained to greatness because of what we are or what we have. We have become the exemplars of all the world because of what we have done with what we are and what we have."[256]

Roosevelt achieved greatness as a leader because he practiced what he preached. He earned the right to lead by exemplifying what he exhorted. And every leader must do the same. He must count the cost of greatness—constant effort and hardship—and then pay it. He must back up his words with action. There is plainly no other path to greatness; surely no other road to leadership.

JUSTICE

If you fail to work in public life, as well as in private, for honesty and
uprightness and virtue, if you condone vice because the vicious man is smart,
or if you in any other way cast your weight into the scales in favor of
evil, you are just so far corrupting and making less valuable
the birthright of your children.[257]

J ustice, an essential element of virtue, is one of the traits desperately wanting in our relativistic and wayward age. There seems to be no end to the political corruption, ministry scandals, and business venality that makes up our daily headlines. Leadership is at an all-time low, and skepticism at an all-time high, when politicians are assumed scoundrels and clergyman are labeled charlatans.

The problem, of course, is that our leaders have lost, amidst the soft sentimentalism of a strange tolerance, the stern moral quality of justice or righteousness. As Roosevelt put it, "The most dangerous form of sentimental debauch is to give expression to good wishes on behalf of virtue while you do nothing about it. Justice is not merely words. It is to be translated into acts."[258]

Roosevelt did not enter politics, however, to be a reformer. Like other aspiring men, he viewed politics as a way to achieve his own ambitions. "When I went into politics at this time," he confessed in his autobiography, "I was not conscious of going in with the set purpose to benefit other people, but of getting for myself a privilege to which I was entitled in common with other people."[259] But a more familiar knowledge of the actual workings of party politics began to open his eyes to the rampant corruption in government, and provoked Roosevelt to labor for the establishment of civic justice. He became a reformer.

During his very first term as a New York assemblyman, Roosevelt contradicted the ruling party bosses by calling on the legislature to investigate the corrupt judicial and civil service systems. In response, the vested interests hired a thug—the boxer Stubby Collins—to beat up Roosevelt. When Collins cornered him outside of a hotel and took a swing at him, Roosevelt knocked him senseless in less than a minute.[260]

From then on, Roosevelt was determined to fight for justice. "Right is right and wrong is wrong. Woe be unto the man who shies away from the battle for justice and righteousness simply because minions of injustice and unrighteousness are arrayed against him."[261]

When Republican Benjamin Harrison won the presidency in 1888, he appointed Roosevelt to fill a position in the Civil Service Commission. For many years previous, the civil service had been a "spoils system" wherein federal jobs were doled out to party supporters. The result was incompetence, inefficiency, and corruption. Roosevelt attacked the system with such vigor that even Harrison complained that Roosevelt "wanted to put an end to all the evil in the world between sunrise and sunset."[262] Not quite, but he did reform the service and establish a merit system for hiring.

Once the civil service was cleaned up, Roosevelt welcomed the new challenge offered to him when recruited to become the police commissioner of New York City in 1895. And a challenge it was. Bribed policemen looked the other way while prostitution, gambling, and racketeering flourished. Moreover, as with the civil service, many appointments were based on political or religious considerations and not on merit. Roosevelt changed all that, of course, by lecturing his men on the need for honesty, courage, vigilance, and energy,[263] and by implementing an examination board to evaluate merit.[264] When Roosevelt submitted his written resignation to the Mayor, he proudly listed some of his accomplishments:

> *For the first time the police force has been administered without regard to politics and with an honest and resolute purpose to enforce the laws equitably and to show favor to no man. The old system of blackmail and corruption has been almost entirely broken up; we have greatly improved the standard of discipline; we have preserved complete order, and we have warred against crime and vice more effectively than ever before.*[265]

Roosevelt's zeal for justice permeated every post he held. Even as the President of the United States, he used the White House as a "bully pulpit" from which to preach his doctrine of personal righteousness and public justice.

> *We must diligently strive to make our young men decent,*
> *God-fearing, law-abiding, honor-loving, justice-doing, and also*
> *fearless and strong, able to hold their own in the hurly-burly*
> *of the world's work, able to strive mightily that the forces of*
> *right may be in the end triumphant. And we must be ever*
> *vigilant in so telling them.*[266]

Roosevelt's critics chafed under his incessant sermons. "Wherever he goes," one detractor complained, "he sets up an impromptu pulpit, and his pious denunciations fall—like the rain and the sunshine upon the just and the unjust—accompanied with a timely warning to the latter to look sharp!"[267] Thomas B. Reed, the Speaker of the House, once quipped that "Roosevelt thought he had discovered the Ten Commandments."[268]

Not exactly; but Roosevelt did believe the Ten Commandments were, and always would be, at the foundation of personal and national prosperity. In his State of the Union address in 1905 he rebuked the advocates of a "new morality" who thought the Decalogue could be replaced because it was obsolete.

> *There are those who believe that a new modernity demands a*
> *new morality. What they fail to consider is the harsh reality*
> *that there is no such thing as a new morality. There is only one*
> *morality. All else is immorality. There is only true Christian*
> *ethics over against which stands the whole of paganism. If we*
> *are to fulfill our great destiny as a people, then we must return*
> *to the old morality, the sole morality.*[269]

The observant editor, William Allen White, correctly summarized Roosevelt's speeches by noting, "Over and over the theme is hammered into the mind and heart of the multitude: Be good, be good, be good; live for righteousness, fight for righteousness, and if need be die for it."[270]

It was fitting, then, when in 1917 as American troops were preparing to hazard the battlefields of France and Belgium in a fight for righteousness, the New York Bible Society asked Roosevelt to inscribe a message in the pocket New Testaments that were to be given to each soldier. In his brief comments on Micah 6:8, Roosevelt summarized the ethic that guided his life and leadership.

> *Do justice; and therefore fight valiantly against those that stand for the reign of Moloch and Beelzebub on this earth. Love mercy; treat your enemies well; succor the afflicted; treat every woman as if she were your sister; care for the little children; and be tender with the old and helpless. Walk humbly; you will do so if you study the life and teachings of the Savior, walking in His steps.*[271]

COURAGE

*Far better it is to dare mighty things, to win glorious triumphs, even
though checkered by failure, than to take rank with those poor spirits who
neither enjoy much nor suffer much because they live in the gray twilight
that knows neither victory nor defeat.*[272]

*T*he life and leadership of Theodore Roosevelt are inexplicable apart from
his hearty dose of courage. While he believed that righteousness was
paramount, it was of no avail in the public arena—the realm of leadership—if
not backed with courage. As he told an audience in Milwaukee in 1910:

> *I don't care how honest a man is, if he is timid he is no good.*
> *I don't want to see a division of our citizenship into good men*
> *who are afraid and bad men who are not at all afraid. The honest*
> *man who is afraid is of just as little use in civic life as in war.*[273]

In his own public service Roosevelt was a courageous reformer who would
not back down to political hacks, entrenched interests, and powerful party
leaders. Fear, he realized, was the death knell of leadership. For that reason he
believed that politicians should never put themselves in the position where
their convictions and livelihood might collide.

> *I do not believe that any man should ever attempt to make*
> *politics his only career. It is a dreadful misfortune for a man to*
> *grow to feel that his whole livelihood and whole happiness*
> *depend upon his staying in office. Such a feeling prevents him*
> *from being of real service to the people while in office and*
> *always puts him under the heaviest strain of pressure to barter*
> *his convictions for the sake of holding office.*[274]

Much to the chagrin of his fainthearted friends, Roosevelt had the impolitic habit of speaking his mind and saying just those things the establishment would resent. Yet he refused to play the pusillanimous politician. "It is absolutely impossible for a Republic long to endure," he declared, "if it becomes either corrupt or cowardly."[275] He would be neither, even though he was denounced, bullied, and his life was threatened.

Roosevelt matched his moral courage with equally astounding physical bravery. In the wilds of Africa he downed a charging rhino closing in at fifty feet, and killed a mountain lion while hanging over a cliff being held at the feet by his guide.

His dauntless exploits in the wild West made Roosevelt's courage legendary in his own day. Once, he entered a hotel in Montana to find a drunken Bad Lander waving a cocked revolver at the frightened guests. Turning toward Roosevelt he shouted, "Four-eyes is going to treat!" The bespectacled Roosevelt laughed, assuming it was a joke. But when the inebriated cowboy approached, pointed the pistol at him, and repeated the demand, Roosevelt abruptly decked him with a powerful right and left to the jaw.[276]

On another occasion, Roosevelt had a showdown with "Hell Roaring" Bill Jones, a man with a short temper and a quick gun. After Bill told a string of filthy stories, Roosevelt rebuked his obscenity. "You're the nastiest-talking man I ever heard," he chided. Bill's hand dropped to his pistol. As others shied away, Roosevelt held his ground. Jones then backed down and apologized, "Mr. Roosevelt. . . I don't mind saying that maybe I've been a little too free with my mouth."[277]

Surprisingly, Roosevelt's courage was not temperamental. It was something he had to learn—the hard way. As a boy he had been "nervous and timid," he tells us in his *Autobiography*. But then one day while visiting Moosehead Lake to recuperate from an asthma attack, a couple of boys bullied him and "industriously proceeded to make life miserable for me." When he tried to fight back he was easily handled. Thereafter, Roosevelt determined "that I would not again be put in such a helpless position." So he made up his mind to learn boxing, build his body, and acquire physical prowess.[278]

Moreover, Roosevelt was inspired to courage by the heroes he read about and admired. Whether it was Washington's soldiers or his Southern forefathers, he tells us, "I felt a great admiration for men who were fearless and who could hold their own in the world, and I had a great desire to be like them."[279]

The greatest test of Roosevelt's courage came when he heard the news that his youngest son, Quentin, had been shot down behind enemy lines during WWI and killed. Paying tribute to his slain son, whom he loved dearly and grieved deeply, Roosevelt said, "Only those are fit to live who do not fear to die; and none are fit to die who have shrunk from the joy of life and the duty of life. Both life and death are part of the same Great Adventure."[280]

Perhaps we could paraphrase this eulogy and say that only those are fit to *lead* who do not fear to die—who do not fear criticism and slander, who do not fear hardship and danger, who do not fear failure and defeat—for each is part of the "Great Adventure" of leadership. Yet the virtue of courage overcomes them all.

ABRAHAM KUYPER
(1837–1920)

Abraham Kuyper was one of the most outstanding leaders of the late nineteenth and early twentieth centuries. Throughout his long life he was a pastor, denominational leader, newspaper editor, theologian, author, statesman, political party leader, and one-time Prime Minister of the Netherlands.

Born in 1837 near Rotterdam, Kuyper studied theology in Leiden and then served as pastor at Beest, Utrecht, and Amsterdam. In 1872 he founded the daily political paper De Standaard (The Standard) *and also served as editor of the weekly religious paper* De Heraut (The Herald).

As a politician Kuyper entered Parliament in 1874 and founded the Anti-Revolutionary Party, made up primarily of Reformed Christians, in 1879. Kuyper's efforts as a statesman culminated in his election as Prime Minister in 1901. As a religious leader Kuyper founded the Free University of Amsterdam in 1880 in order to provide students with a thoroughly reformed life and worldview. Moreover, in response to the liberal clergy, Kuyper led a secession from the Dutch Reformed Church to found the strictly orthodox Reformed Free Church of the Netherlands.

Kuyper was also a prolific writer and persuasive speaker. Many of his devotionals, originally written for The Herald, *have been published in book form. In addition he wrote works on theology* (Encyclopaedia of Sacred Theology: Its Principles; The Work of the Holy Spirit; *and others*), *Biblical exposition* (The Revelation of St. John; The Practice of Godliness), *and socio-political issues* (Christianity and the Class Struggle; Our Program). *Unfortunately, many of his written works are not available in English.*

In October 1898, at the height of his fame, Kuyper was invited to Princeton Seminary to give the "Stone Lectures," for which he was awarded an honorary doctorate by Princeton University. Those lectures were the fruit of thirty years of rigorous research and reflection on the meaning of Christianity in an age of religious unbelief and moral relativism. Subsequently published as Lectures on Calvinism, *Kuyper's comprehensive world- and lifeview continues to challenge Christians to acknowledge the Lordship of Christ over every sphere of life.*

WORLDVIEW

In the total expanse of human life there is not a single square inch of which Christ, who alone is sovereign, does not declare, "That is mine!"[281]

O ne of the striking facts of Abraham Kuyper's leadership is that he was a leader in several major fields simultaneously. He maintained separate, yet related, careers in politics, church, the academy, and the press. He was both a thinker and a doer; a builder and a battler; a wise man and a warrior.

His prodigious accomplishments in separate fields were a product not simply of Kuyper's genius and energy (both of which were great), but more importantly they reflected the comprehensive nature of his worldview. In addition to having a clear vision of his objectives in each field, (as should every leader) he also was able to see and articulate a broad view of the various areas of life based on fundamental principles.

Thus it is fair to say that it is impossible to understand Kuyper's career apart from the importance he attached to the subject of worldview. According to him, everyone holds certain presuppositions or principles that determine their view of life. The German term for this outlook is *Weltanschauung,* which has no exact English equivalent, but has been translated "view of the world." Kuyper often used the words "life and worldview" or "life system" synonymously.

But what exactly did he mean by these terms? In his famous "Stone Lectures" on Calvinism, Kuyper stated that a world-view must satisfy three conditions. "These conditions demand in the first place, that from a special principle a peculiar insight be obtained into the three fundamental relations of all human life: namely, one, our relation to God; two, our relation to man; and three, our relation to the world."[282] It was Kuyper's bold contention that Calvinism meets these three conditions and imparts a meaningful and coherent explanation to our relation to God, man, and the world.

First, Calvinism postulates that man may have immediate access to God through the cross of Christ and the present operation of the Holy Spirit in regeneration and sanctification. This "fundamental interpretation of the immediate fellowship with God," contrary to Rome's clericalism and Modernism's skepticism, means "the whole of man's life is to be lived as in the Divine Presence. . ."[283]

Secondly, Calvinism defines our relationship to our fellowman. "If Calvinism places our entire human life immediately before God, then it follows that all men or women, rich or poor, weak or strong, dull or talented, as creatures of God, and as lost sinners, have no claim whatsoever to lord over one another, and that we stand as equal before God. . ."[284] Thus the immortal glory of Calvinism in its social aspect is that it "placed man on a footing of equality with man, so far as the purely human interests are concerned. . ."[285]

This does not mean, however, that there are no distinctions among men. Kuyper acknowledged that "there is no uniformity among men" and that the act of creation established differences of sex and talent. Equality must not be confused with uniformity, which is precisely the deadening error of Modernism.

> *Finally Modernism, which denies and abolishes every difference, cannot rest until it has made woman man and man woman, and, putting every distinction on a common level, kills life by placing it under the ban of uniformity. One type must answer for all, one uniform, one position and one and the same development of life; and whatever goes beyond and above it, is looked upon as an insult to the common consciousness.*[286]

Thirdly, Calvinism sees the world as a Divine creation rather than a product of evolution; and as such God works in the world through common grace so that man may fulfill the original cultural mandate to exercise dominion over the earth. As Kuyper put it, Calvinism recognizes "that in the whole world the curse is restrained by grace, that the life of the world is to be honored in its independence, and that we must, in every domain, discover the treasures and develop the potencies hidden by God in nature and in human life."[287]

At the heart of Kuyper's worldview, of course, was the Sovereign God, who not only created all things, but was the ever-present Lord of Creation. This simple theological truth, admitted by all true Christians, was for Kuyper a revelation pregnant with implications for every area of life. If Christ is Lord then His Lordship must not be limited to the institutional Church but must equally be declared and expressed in every aspect of our lives. Christians must "glorify their King in all areas of life."[288] There is no neutral ground, no area where Christ is not present and sovereign. Thus, Christians are called to labor for Christ outside the Church in the realms of the family, education, politics, media, science, the arts—indeed, in every sphere of human activity.

Nothing better summarizes the implications of Kuyper's worldview than the following quotation from his lectures on Calvinism.

> *God is present in all life with the influence of his omnipresent and almighty power, and no sphere of human life is conceivable in which religion does not maintain its demands that God shall be praised, that God's ordinances shall be observed, and that every labora shall be permeated with its ora in fervent and ceaseless prayer. Wherever man may stand, whatever he may do, to whatever he may apply his hand, in agriculture, in commerce, and in industry, or his mind, in the world of art, and science, he is, in whatsoever it may be, constantly standing before the face of his God, he is employed in the service of his God, he has strictly to obey his God, and above all, he has to aim at the glory of his God.[289]*

This vision of a universal application of Christian duty to serve and glorify God was the real source of Kuyper's monumental achievements as a scholar, statesman, and seer. His worldview was not an abstraction but a plan of action. Moreover, men followed him because of the inspiration that comes from a noble and grand vision of life. As one of his biographers correctly noted:

> *Kuyper did not rest until he had developed his views on an all-comprehensive life- and worldview, with the Calvinistic thought of the absolute sovereignty of God as its core, into a well rounded-out scientific system. He was an encyclopedic*

man of learning for whom the moral world order itself, and not so much the details of the visible creation, formed the object of his investigation. It is one of his greatest merits that he inspired something of that sense for the universal in the souls of that common rank and file, whose leader he was for many, many years.[290]

PRINCIPLE

If the battle is to be fought with honor and with a hope of victory, then principle must be arrayed against principle; then it must be felt that in Modernism the vast energy of an all-embracing life system assails us, then also it must be understood that we have to take our stand in a life system of equally comprehensive and far-reaching power.[291]

One of the differences between a charlatan and a leader is that the charlatan postures in public while the leader is planted on principle. Indeed, in the political realm—the arena in which Kuyper spent the majority of his life—the difference between a mere politician and a true statesman is that a politician will waffle on his policies while a statesman will hold to his convictions. A true leader, and a true statesman, will not be swayed by the currents of public opinion, nor retreat in the face of criticism, but will be true to his deepest convictions despite rejection.

As we have seen, Abraham Kuyper's multifaceted leadership was a reflection of his comprehensive worldview. His worldview, however, was really nothing more than a systematic development of seminal principles. The basic principles of Christianity, or Calvinism, as Kuyper would have preferred, were thought out and articulated in such a way that one could make sense of the totality of life and fulfill one's vocation in a principled manner.

To Kuyper, principle was everything. Why? Because, as he said, "As truly as every plant has a root, so truly does a principle hide under every manifestation of life."[292] And from the basic principles of one's thought, as manifested in action, there grows a comprehensive worldview. "These principles are interconnected, and have their common root in a fundamental principle; and from the latter is developed logically and systematically the whole complex of ruling ideas and conceptions that go to make up our life and world-view."[293]

As a Christian leader Kuyper labored to awake the church to the importance of principles. That is one reason why he refused to formally fellowship with those churchmen who denied the inspiration of the Scriptures. And that is also why he challenged the church of his day to avoid the "tactics of the ostrich," by which he meant the attempt to avoid the inevitable conflict between worldviews—especially the conflict between Modernism and Christianity. To those who thought that they could hold on to their theology without applying Biblical principles to other areas of life, Kuyper replied, "To confine yourself to the saving of your upper room, when the rest of the house in on fire, is foolish indeed."[294]

Unfortunately, many Christians avoid dealing with the reality of conflict by either finding solace in mysticism or losing themselves in the bustle of "practical" Christianity. Kuyper challenged these escapists by reminding them that the historic church bravely faced persecution only because it was willing to take its stand on principle.

> *Mysticism is sweet, and Christian works are precious, but the seed of the Church, both at the birth of Christianity and in the age of the Reformation, has been the blood of martyrs; and our sainted martyrs shed their blood not for mysticism and not for philanthropic projects, but for the sake of convictions such as concerned the acceptance of truth and the rejection of error.*[295]

Thus the only defense against a comprehensive onslaught is a principled and comprehensive counterattack.

> *With such a coherent world and life-view, firmly resting on its principle and self-consistent in its splendid structure, Modernism now confronts Christianity; and against this deadly danger, ye, Christians, cannot successfully defend your sanctuary, but by placing, in opposition to all this, a life and world-view of your own, founded as firmly on the base of your own principle, wrought out with the same clearness and glittering in an equally logical consistency.*[296]

When forming the Anti-Revolutionary Party, Kuyper insisted that the party be committed to a clearly enunciated set of principles. In fact, he spent nearly the entire decade of the 1870's working on what came to be called the "Anti-Revolutionary Program," which contained twenty-one principles that applied revealed or Biblical norms to the problems of the times.[297] And in both *The Standard* and *The Herald* Kuyper tirelessly strove to show the abiding relevance of these same Biblical principles.

Throughout his political career, Kuyper insisted on expounding and debating principles rather than simply arguing over particular proposals. "If attention is given to principles," he wrote in April 1875, "then you will have the ear of the nation."[298] Biblical principles were normative for all of life, including politics. Thus his foundational principle was a firm commitment to Scriptural infallibility. Moral principles derived from the Bible were applicable to modern society and the State. Although he rejected any theocratic imposition of the Mosaic civil law, he did recognize that the Decalogue was morally binding on all men. The State is bound to God's ordinances through the consciences of magistrates and voters, however, not through the edicts of a State church.

When Kuyper was elected as Prime Minister of the Netherlands, he made clear to Parliament that he intended to govern according to Christian principles. In spite of rumors of "theocratic oppression," Kuyper insisted on clearly delineating the difference between Christianity and Humanism in politics. For instance, during the Great Railroad Strike of 1903, Kuyper addressed the House thus:

> *The recent discussion in this Chamber concerns the nature of law. But a basic difficulty arises when God is eliminated from law since legal certainty also vanishes. . . There must be a higher authority than written law; this is the question that is presently being debated. . . In response to Troelstra and Marx, we Christians say that the standard for law is not found in men, but that the idea of law comes from God. But because man is created in God's image, he too, has an idea of the highest law that is universally valid as determined by God's control over the world. It has been asked why we also oppose the Liberal when the Socialists have caused the present danger. My response is that neither Anti-Revolutionaries nor Catholics will limit their struggle to merely opposing Social Democrats because in doing so they*

would lose their own distinctive principles. The great antithesis between Liberal and what they term "clericals" is that the Liberal ignore God's revelation. We derive revelation not only from the Holy Scriptures but also from nature and reason while recognizing that the defects of nature and reason must have the necessary corrective of Special Revelation.[299]

As is clear from this representative statement, Kuyper's custom was to stand not on human policy but on divine principle. And like all great leaders, he accomplished good in the world because he looked for the world to come. Knowing that one day he would stand before Christ, he stood on Christ's word, the foundation of all true principle.

CRITICISM

*Radical determination must be insisted upon. Half-measure cannot guarantee
the desired result. Superficiality will not brace us for the conflict.
Principle must again bear witness against principle, world-view against
world-view, spirit against spirit.*[300]

C riticism is one of most painful yet inevitable tests of leadership.
Leadership is not, as some would like to think, a popularity contest. It
is not about pleasing people, striving to be liked, or attempting to gain
admiration. Rather, leadership is about making the hard decisions despite
the competing claims and wishes of others. It means acting conscientiously
even though it will engender hostility. It means standing on principle when
tempted to compromise for the sake of peace or unity.

As we have seen, Kuyper was a man committed to principle. He was
willing to fearlessly declare the obvious antithesis between Humanism
and Christianity, idolatry and worship. The modern tendency to ignore fundamental differences, and suggest that tolerance and cooperation are virtues in
themselves, was anathema to him. He understood that while it is true that
"Blessed are the peacemakers;" it is also true that there can be no authentic
peace between truth and error, faith and unbelief, light and darkness.

As a result, Kuyper was throughout his life, as both a churchman and
politician, severely criticized. Within the church, Kuyper was intent on point-
ing out the danger—indeed, the anti-Christian nature—of the liberal theology
that was then widespread in the Netherlands. For instance, in March of 1871,
he delivered a lecture entitled, "Modernism a Fata Morgana in the Realm of
Christianity." The Fata Morgana is an exceptional aerial phenomenon that
occurs in the Strait of Messina and other places nearby, in which houses,
palaces, towers, and even entire cities appear high in the sky. Essentially an
aerial mirage, the Fata Morgana is majestic, beautiful, and captivating—yet
it is false. It is an illusion. The same is true of Liberal theology, said Kuyper.
It is devoid of reality. While using Christian terminology, Liberalism denies
the essential truths of the faith.[301]

With biting sarcasm, Kuyper defined the Liberal Creed:

I believe in a God who is the Father of all men, and Jesus—not the Christ but the rabbi of Nazareth. I believe in man who is good by nature and must only press on to become perfect. I believe that sin is only a relative matter, and that forgiveness of sins is therefore only a human invention. I believe in the hope of a better life, and in the salvation of all souls, without judgment.[302]

Kuyper's unremitting challenge to Liberalism in the church, and his outspoken advocacy for a genuinely reformed church, led eventually to the secession and formation of the orthodox Dutch Reformed Church. For this he was bitterly denounced as a "rebel" and "schismatic." He even received life-threatening letters. The hostility was so intense that the police offered to provide him a bodyguard. But Kuyper replied, "I place my life in the hand of God."[303]

Kuyper's political career was no less tumultuous. His reputation as an Anti-Revolutionary preceded him, and Parliament did not receive him with open arms. During his first term certain liberals mockingly called him "Dominee," and according to one author "strove to outdo each other in inventing abusive language to be directed against him."[304] As his biographer Vanden Berg has noted:

For Kuyper the two years in Parliament were a baptism in fire. To the great majority in the Second Chamber, he was not a popular man. Some spoke of a "whited sepulcher." Others accused him of the design to overthrow the monarch, establish a republic, and set himself up as another Cromwell. The opposition, arrogant and bitter, sometimes resorted to tactics that violated all common courtesy and Parliamentary good form. Newspapers and magazines, too, attacked him viciously.[305]

Liberal hatred for Kuyper (which was really hatred of his Christian principles) reached its peak when he became Prime Minister in 1901. Because he faithfully pointed out the principled antithesis between Humanism and Christianity in politics, his political enemies continually leveled false charges against him. His Cabinet was charged with being inept, while he himself was called a "political manipulator" and "anti-democratic," by which his opponents maliciously implied his was scheming to set up a "theocracy."[306]

When Kuyper was up for re-election in 1905, all the liberal forces joined together to crush him. They hated him with a perfect hatred, and made him "the issue" of the campaign. According to Vanden Berg, "In this 1905 campaign, the important, the paramount, the only issue was Kuyper. The opposition organized a crusade against the Kuyper cabinet, more especially, the Prime Minister himself. 'Out with Kuyper!' was the unwritten plank in all their platforms. . . To them Kuyper was anathema, the archenemy."[307]

> *Anti-Kuyper speakers traveled through the country with feverish activity. They worked themselves into a peculiar frenzy. Their voices became hoarse and foggy as they orated in misty, sepulchral tones. Others, in unparalleled bitterness, vilified and flayed Kuyper mercilessly. Half-truths, manifest distortion and twisting of the truth, inflammatory denunciation, pure demagoguery, harsh epithets, savage attacks were their stock in trade. All their pent-up wrath exploded against him. The scurrilous campaign conducted by the Left still stands as an unexampled prostitution of political morality.*[308]

The hate campaign of 1905 succeeded, and Kuyper was defeated—defeated as Prime Minister, but not defeated as a leader. For although his enemies unethically used any means possible to defeat him, Kuyper would not lower himself to the level of his opponents. There is no doubt that he was greatly disappointed by his loss, but he would not succumb to bitterness or retaliate with slander or libel. He was simply too great a man for that. What he did do, however, was to continue in the right path. He maintained his principles and continued to espouse them in both public and private, placing both his life and reputation in the hands of the Sovereign God whom he professed, and for whom he was severely and unjustly treated.

Hence, in his principled response to criticism, as well as in other aspects of his character, Kuyper serves as a model for our generation of leaders.

G. K. CHESTERTON
(1874–1936)

Gilbert Keith Chesterton was a poet, playwright, novelist, art and literary critic, biographer, essayist, and, above all, a journalist and Christian apologist.

Born on Campden Hill, London, Chesterton was raised in a progressively Evangelical home and first educated at St. Paul's School, where he was the class dunce. His knack for drawing was observed by his teachers, however, so he was then sent to the Slade School of Art while also studying literature at London University.

G.K.'s early career was in publishing, and from there he drifted into journalism, where he remained for the rest of his life. Throughout his journalistic career, Chesterton worked for the Daily News, the Speaker, the Illustrated London News, and edited his own paper, G.K.'s Weekly. In these and other publications Chesterton made a career of attacking the follies of modernism, such as materialist philosophy, evolutionary theory, scientific determinism, socialism, collectivism, eugenics, and the myth of progress. Enjoying the life of a Fleet Street journalist, Chesterton made friends with such British notables as Hillaire Belloc, H. G. Wells, and George Bernard Shaw.

Chesterton's literary output was prodigious (over ninety books) and varied. Many of his articles and essays were published as books such as Tremendous Trifles and All Is Grist. His better known novels included The Ball and the Cross, The Flying Inn, and The Man Who Was Thursday, while his criticism and biography covered Robert Browning, Charles Dickens and others. Chesterton also wrote several plays ("Magic" and "The Judgment of Dr. Johnson"), detective stories (The Innocence of Father Brown), history (Short History of England), social philosophy (Heretics, What's Wrong With the World?), and Christian apologetics (Orthodoxy, The Everlasting Man).

In all his work, Chesterton displayed a winsome wit and wisdom that won him the admiration of even his philosophical opponents, and makes him still one of the most often quoted writers of our age. And in all, he maintained the sanity of orthodox Christianity against the madness of modern heresy.

HUMOR

Why is it funny that a man should sit down suddenly in the street? There is only one possible or intelligent reason: that man is the image of God... Why do we laugh? Because it is a grave religious matter: it is the Fall of Man. Only man can be absurd: for only man can be dignified.[309]

H umor is a virtue we do not normally associate with leadership. Courage? Yes. Vision? Unquestionably. But humor? Yet it is striking how many great leaders—men like Churchill, Wilberforce, Henry, and others—had a sharp wit and keen sense of irony. This undoubtedly reflects, amongst other things, a leader's depth of insight. As Samuel Johnson once noted, "The size of a man's understanding might be justly measured by his mirth."[310] And just as a leader must be a man of insight and wisdom, so he will also be a man of mirth.

Chesterton was, of course, a master jokester, reveling in puns, paradoxes, and playfulness. And it was his humor, as much as his profound acumen, that made him such a popular author and entertaining speaker, earning him such titles as the "Capering Humorist," the "Metaphysical Jester," and "Chesterton the Child."

Growing up in the Gilded Age, the formal creed of the times (at least before W.W.I) was a facile optimism built on a vague belief in "progress." The bursts of scientific discoveries and technological inventions heralded the dawning of a new millennium of peace and prosperity. The Shavian Superman would usher in a secular utopia—a humanist's paradise revolving on the wheels of science and ruled by a master race.

Chesterton knew better, however; for underneath the golden glitter of modern technology was the rusting ore of nihilist philosophy. Though the Gilded Age was superficially optimistic, it was in fact a castle in the air with no moral or theological foundation. "God is dead!" cried Nietsche. And Shaw rejoiced that Superman cometh. Following Darwin, H.G. Wells outlined the ascent of man and Spencer triumphed the "survival of the fittest." The world became God's graveyard, and the ghosts of materialism, determinism, socialism, and eugenics haunted young intellectuals, Chesterton among them. They were aimless and brooding. The pall of pessimism that draped God's casket descended upon their minds. As Chesterton put it in one of his notebooks, "It might strike many persons as strange that in a time on the whole so optimistic in its intellectual beliefs as this is, in an age when only a small minority disbelieve in social progress, and a large majority believe in an ultimate social perfection, there should be such a tired and blasé feeling among numbers of young men."[311]

After a dark night of the soul, wherein Chesterton reflected on the madness of modernity, and dreamed of violence and suicide, he awoke from the nightmare with joy in his heart and a chuckle in his mouth. It is unclear if he was converted at this time, but it is certain that through much anguish of spirit he came to see the world from a fundamentally Christian point of view. From that point on, Chesterton regarded the Christian worldview as the essence of sanity.[312]

Viewing man as the creation of God, Chesterton now could appreciate true humor, because humor was fundamentally theological. As he said, "All jokes about men sitting down on their hats are really theological jokes; they are concerned with the Dual Nature of Man. They refer to the primary paradox that man is superior to all the things around him and yet is at their mercy."[313]

Not only is man a created being but he is also a fallen being; he must learn to laugh in order to reprove his pride. "It is unpardonable conceit not to laugh at your own jokes," Chesterton once remarked. "Joking is undignified; that is why it is good for one's soul. Do not fancy you can be a detached wit and avoid being a buffoon; you cannot. If you are the Court Jester you must be the Court Fool."[314]

Chesterton, himself, had no problem playing the buffoon. In fact, in an age suffering from modern madness, a great and sane man might in fact appear the buffoon. It all depends on one's perspective.

When corruption and chaos are disturbing ordinary minds, and many good men are only worried and serious, it has often happened that a great man could apparently be frivolous; and appear in history almost as a great buffoon. . . And there is always

something about them puzzling to those who see their frivolity
from the outside and not their faith from the inside. It is not
realized that their faith is not a stagnation but an equilibrium.[315]

Accordingly, Chesterton took humor seriously.[316] For him it was both a theological deduction and a journalistic weapon. It was a conscious effort on his part to appreciate the grand gift of life and to protest the secular forces in modern life that sought to dehumanize and discourage man. Joy was a gift of God, but now that God was dead, man was unhappy. Killing God meant, in the end, murdering man.

There is a sense in which men may be made normally happy;
but there is another sense in which we may truly say, without
undue paradox, that what they want is to get back to their
normal unhappiness. At present they are suffering from an utterly
abnormal unhappiness. They have got all the tragic elements
essential to the human lot to contend with; time and death and
bereavement and unrequited affection and dissatisfaction with
themselves. But they have not got the elements of consolation
and encouragement that ought normally to renew their hopes or
restore their self-respect. They have not got vision or conviction,
or the mastery of their work, or the loyalty of their household, or
any form of human dignity.[317]

Throughout his career Chesterton would make such amusing comments as, "The Bible tells us to love our neighbors, and also to love our enemies, probably because they are generally the same people."[318] Or, "The best way to destroy a Utopia is to establish it."[319] After visiting America Chesterton once quipped to the press, "I do not plan to go farther west than Chicago, for having seen Jerusalem and Chicago, I think I shall have touched the extremes of civilization."[320] And upon being dazzled by the lights of Broadway, "What a glorious garden of wonders this would be to anyone who was lucky enough not to be able to read."[321]

Beneath Chesterton's outward displays of humor there was a profound insight, keen observation, and a deep concern for his fellow man. It is fair to say that without these qualities one cannot attain leadership. And that is why humor, strange as it first sounds, is a sure mark of a sound leader.

HUMILITY

Humility is a grand, a stirring thing, the exalting paradox of Christianity, and the sad want of it in our own time is, we believe, what really makes us think life dull, like a cynic, instead of marvelous, like a child.[322]

One of the myths surrounding leadership is that a leader is a confident swaggart, self-conscious of his own greatness. Perhaps this error is generated by all the modern drivel about self-esteem and assertiveness that one finds in popular self-help books. Or possibly it is our tendency to imagine that a leader thinks of himself in the same way that we, in our admiration, esteem him.

In either case, the actual truth is that humility and greatness are coincidental. As Jesus said, "He that would be great must be the servant of all."[323] And elsewhere, "Whosoever therefore shall humble himself as this little child, the same is greatest in the kingdom of heaven."[324]

Chesterton rightly perceived the nature of humility when he noted that modern man suffers from what he called a "dislocation of humility."

> *But what we suffer from to-day is humility in the wrong place. Modesty has moved from the organ of ambition. Modesty has settled upon the organ of conviction; where it was never meant to be. A man was meant to be doubtful about himself, but undoubting about the truth; this has been exactly reversed. Nowadays the part of a man that a man does assert is exactly the part he ought not to assert—himself. The part he doubts is exactly the part he ought not to doubt—Divine Reason.[325]*

Believing in one's self, or what today is called self-esteem, is a sign not of strength but of weakness, not of greatness but of smallness. It is a form of idolatry that worships a very small god—the solitary self! Its altar is the bathroom mirror.

On one occasion when a publisher commented to Chesterton that so and so would "get on" because "he believes in himself," Chesterton replied:

> *If you consulted your business experience instead of your ugly individualistic philosophy, you would know that believing in himself is one of the commonest signs of a rotter. Actors who can't act believe in themselves; and debtors who won't pay. It would be much truer to say that a man will certainly fail, because he believes in himself. Complete self-confidence is not merely a sin; complete self-confidence is a weakness. Believing utterly in one's self is a hysterical and superstitious belief. . .* [326]

The irony of popular psychology's morbid preoccupation with "high self-esteem" and a "positive self-image" is that it utterly fails to make one happy or successful. Chesterton saw this and commented, "Whereas it has been supposed that the fullest possible enjoyment is to be found by extending our ego to infinity, the truth is that the fullest possible enjoyment is to be found by reducing our ego to zero." [327] Why is this so? Because humility "was largely meant as a restraint upon the arrogance and infinity of the appetite of man," said Chesterton. "He was always outstripping his mercies with his own newly invented needs. His very power of enjoyment destroyed half his joys. By asking for pleasure, he lost the chief pleasure; for the chief pleasure is surprise." [328]

Thus the key to happiness, as well as greatness, lies in humility—"the exalting paradox of Christianity." It is a paradox because it rests on the apparently sad doctrine of original sin. Yet as one of G.K.'s friends once commented, "Well, anyhow, it must be obvious to anybody that the doctrine of the fall is the only cheerful view of human life." [329] For only when a man acknowledges his sin can he then choose to humble himself before God and enjoy the renewal and refreshment of repentance.

Chesterton, of course, chose the Christian low road of humility, and learned to view the world through the eyes of a child—the eyes of wonder and gratitude. "The truth is," he quipped, "Blessed is he that expecteth nothing, for he shall be gloriously surprised."[330] His joy and appreciation for life were displayed in his overflowing humor (especially his ability to laugh at himself), and the fact that he maintained friendships with his theological adversaries. As one biographer put it, "He excelled in the soft answer. . . In the heat of argument he retained a fairness of mind that saw his opponent's case and would never turn an argument into a quarrel. And most people liked him and felt that he liked them."[331]

Indeed, most people did like Chesterton, his popularity in large measure resulting from his humility. By the time he was thirty, he was already famous in England, and his fame grew with his age. His public debates with his nemesis, George Bernard Shaw, were always well attended; and when Chesterton gave lectures throughout Europe or America he was a smashing success. Writing in the person of one of his well-beloved characters, Father Brown, Chesterton recalls his reception in New York:

> When Father Brown first stepped off an Atlantic liner on to American soil, he discovered. . . that he was a much more important person than he had ever supposed. . . America has a genius for the encouragement of fame. . . and he found himself held up on the quay by a group of journalists, as by a gang of brigands, who asked him questions about all the subjects on which he was least likely to regard himself as an authority, such as the details of female dress and the criminal statistics of the country that he had only the moment clapped his eye on.[332]

When a reporter asked him which of his works he thought was the greatest, Chesterton replied with his characteristic humility, "I don't consider any of my works in the least great."[333]

It is precisely because Chesterton cared little for fame and was lacking in self-consciousness that he was willing to contradict the prevailing ideologies of his age. His humility made him brave for battle. And like other great leaders, he was willing to sacrifice his reputation for the sake of truth, and to be counted a fool for Christ.

PATRIOTISM

The unreasonable patriot is one who sees the faults of his fatherland with an eye which is clearer and more merciless than any eye of hatred, the eye of an irrational and irrevocable love.[334]

*C*hesterton's popularity did not exempt him from criticism—indeed, it never does, especially when a leader is challenging the predominate predilections of his times. And that is exactly what Chesterton attempted to do. In fact, his continual opposition to industrialism, imperialism, and jingoism brought against him the charge of being unpatriotic.

For instance, the Boer War, which broke out between the Dutch and British in South Africa in 1899, had its roots in the imperialistic expansion of many European countries (England among them) during the nineteenth century. From the 1870's to the first decade of the 20th century, Great Britain extended its power over vast colonies throughout Africa and the Orient. In just six years under Prime Minister Disraeli, Britain annexed Fiji and Cypress, battled the native population in parts of Africa, acquired shares in the Suez Canal, and named Queen Victoria as the "Empress of India." The sun never set on the British Empire since the empire circled the globe: Egypt, Somaliland, Bechuanaland, East Africa, South Africa, Sudan, Gambia, Sierra Leone, Gold Coast, Persia, India, New Zealand, Australia, Canada, and elsewhere.

In South Africa, the Boers, who were Dutch, had originally colonized the area and had established two independent states—Transvaal and Orange Free State—far from British control. However, when gold was discovered in Transvaal, many foreigners (or Uitlanders as they were called) flooded the state in search of wealth. Meanwhile, the British capitalist Cecil Rhodes schemed to overthrow the government of Transvaal, and when the plot failed, war broke out between Britain and the Boers.

Popular patriotism in England tended to equate colonial empire building—or what Chesterton called imperialism—with patriotism; and thus most Englishmen instinctively but uncritically supported the war. Chesterton, however, demurred. Rather, "it seemed obvious that Patriotism and

Imperialism were not only not the same thing, but very nearly opposite things."[335] To Chesterton, imperialism was "the attempt of a European country to create a kind of sham Europe which it can dominate, instead of the real Europe, which it can only share."[336] Because imperialism entailed the unlawful domination of a people, it not only hurt the oppressed but also harmed the oppressor. It was morally degrading to England to engage in villainous oppression and unjust warfare, which was why Chesterton referred to imperialism as a "running sore" in the nation.[337]

According to Chesterton's friend Belloc, G.K. "suffered at any word against England" because "his patriotism was passionate."[338] Yet Chesterton felt himself duty bound to criticize his beloved country when he believed that his country was wrong. And in this Chesterton showed that he understood the true nature of patriotism. Contrary to such shallow slogans as "My country right or wrong,"—a slogan used to justify the Boer War—Chesterton replied in his characteristically witty way:

> *My country, right or wrong, is a thing no patriot would think of saying, except in a desperate case. It is like saying "my mother, drunk or sober." No doubt if a decent man's mother took to drink he would share her troubles to the last; but to talk as if he would be in a state of gay indifference as to whether his mother took to drink or not is certainly not the language of men.*[339]

True patriotism, then, does not mean "my country right or wrong" but rather "my country make it right." As one author put it, Chesterton "could not wave the flag and cheer when his country was in the wrong."[340] A real patriot will appreciate his country's traditions, language, and institution. This is true, but not at the expense of truth and righteousness.

Nor does patriotism mean "my country the bigger the better," which is the essence of imperialism and the heart of greed. Chesterton's ideal was rather "an England territorially small, spiritually great,"[341] which is just the opposite of imperialism. If one's country is not morally upright and spiritually sound, what is there to export? What's the point in spreading decadence?

As in the case of the Boer War, G.K. took a similarly unpopular stand against England's attempt to incorporate Ireland into Great Britain. Contrary to many of his countrymen he came out in favor of home rule for Ireland. Why? Because, as he said, "I have always felt it the first duty of a real English patriot to sympathize with the passionate patriotism of Ireland."[342] What we see here again is Chesterton's clear understanding of true patriotism. It is, in effect, not merely the love of one's country but more importantly the love of local tradition and freedom, and is thus opposed to the modern trend, so evident in Chesterton's day as in our own, toward centralization. In fact, the historical meaning of the word patriotism is love of one's ancestry or fatherland as opposed to one's king or government. So instead of patriotism being a blind obedience to governmental authority, or an uncritical veneration of the State, it actually entails resistance to distant control in the quest for local liberty.

In order to have liberty, however, more is needed than simple decentralization. Liberty requires property. Chesterton understood this, and thus advocated an economic scheme called distributism. As the name implies, distributism required that every man had a right to a small amount of property as a defense to his liberty and a mark of his dignity. The family is the foundation of society, yet the family could never be free without property. By recommending distributism, Chesterton stood against the collectivism of both industrialism and socialism. In the opening issue of his distributist paper, *G.K.'s Weekly*, Chesterton put it like this:

> *This single adventure in weekly journalism cannot compete with our wealthy and world-wide press in resources and reports. But it exists to demand that we fight Bolshevism [i.e. Socialism] with something better than plutocracy [i.e. capitalism]. . . The thing behind Bolshevism. . . is a new doubt. . . not merely a doubt about God, it is rather specially a doubt about man. The old morality, the Christian religion. . . really believed in the rights of man. . . These [new] sages cannot trust the normal man to rule in the home; and most certainly do not want him to rule in the State. . . They are not willing to give him a house, or a wife or a child or a dog, or a cow or a piece of land; because these things really do give him power. . . That is what we think; and Bolshevism and Capitalism are absolutely at one in thinking the opposite.*[343]

Chesterton correctly perceived that imperialism, socialism, and industrial capitalism all tended toward unification and centralization on a large scale. The result was a loss of liberty and the much graver loss of dignity. In his *Autobiography* Chesterton noted the link between liberty and dignity:

> *It was my instinct to defend liberty in small nations and poor families; that is, to defend the rights of man as including the rights of property; especially the property of the poor. I did not really understand what I meant by Liberty, until I heard it called by the name of Human Dignity.*[344]

Chesterton's patriotism avoided the extremes of jingoism or imperialism because it was rooted in creationism. He could love his country, that is, his local customs and traditions—and yes his "little England"—but not if it required dehumanizing other peoples. Every man has dignity because he is the handiwork of God. And we should likewise recognize that each man's traditions are as precious to him as ours are to us.

Moreover, Chesterton's patriotism was undoubtedly an important factor in keeping him in journalism his entire life, although he could have probably spent his later years writing "literature." For it was in his role as a journalist that Chesterton sought to change his world for the better. In other words, patriotism is an active virtue. It requires involvement with our culture. It is opposed to false piety—that withdrawal from all "worldly" social or political issues, which marks so many modern churches. In a sense, we might say that real patriotism is an application or expression of the second great commandment to love our neighbor as ourselves; for without active involvement in our community we display a callous disregard for our neighbor's welfare.

So, while genuine patriotism entails a love of ancestry and fatherland, it also entails the higher love of people: family, friends, and neighbors. This is the ultimate test, not only of one's patriotism, but also of one's leadership. For how a leader treats people is the true sign of his character.

C. S. LEWIS
(1898–1963)

C. S. Lewis was born in Belfast, the second of two boys. His mother died when he was a child of nine, and Lewis was then sent off to a number of dreary boarding schools. After being rescued by his father, Lewis was tutored by W. T. Kirkpatrick, whose instruction shaped Lewis for the rest of his life. In 1916 Lewis won a classical scholarship to Oxford and began the life of a scholar.

After a brief stint in the military during W.W.I, he returned to Oxford and in 1925 was elected as a fellow and tutor in English language and literature, a post he held for nearly thirty years. In 1956 Magdalen College persuaded him to accept the newly created chair in English medieval and Renaissance literature established at Cambridge. While at Magdalen, Lewis met weekly with a few friends, known as the Inklings, for fellowship, scholarly discussion and readings, and just plain fun. Amongst the Inklings were J.R.R. Tolkien, Nevill Coghill, Owen Barfield, Charles Williams, and others. Lewis also established the Socratic Club in 1942 for scholarly debate between Christians and skeptics. He served as its president until 1954.

Lewis was a first rate Christian scholar and the successor of G.K. Chesterton as the lay apostle to modernity. Although he wrote several scholarly works that brought him acclaim (The Allegory of Love; English Literature in the Sixteenth Century; An Experiment in Criticism), *Lewis' lasting fame is the fruit of his many explicitly Christian works, especially those that are apologetic in nature* (Mere Christianity; Miracles; The Problem of Pain). *His* Screwtape Letters, *a fictitious account of senior devil training a younger tempter, was and still is, one of Lewis' most popular books. His children's books,* The Chronicles of Narnia, *are considered by some to be classics in that field. Lewis also wrote poetry, essays, science fiction, and other popular works.*

He emphatically spoke the truth, but always spoke in love. And was able to argue the case for reasonable righteousness better than any other Christian thinker of the twentieth century. Throughout all his works, but mainly in his popular books, Lewis displayed a profound logic, a warm affability, a dry wit, and a simple humility that continues to endear him to popular audiences.

LEARNING

It has always . . . been one of my main endeavours as a teacher to persuade the young that first-hand knowledge is not only more worth acquiring than second-hand knowledge, but is usually much easier and more delightful to acquire.[345]

C S. Lewis once described himself in a letter to a young admirer, "I'm tall, fat, rather bald, red-faced, double-chinned, black-haired, have a deep voice, and wear glasses for reading."[346] With such a droll and derogatory description, one might object to Lewis' place in a pantheon of leaders.

The objection, however, is really based on the tacit assumption that leadership always requires physical action (versus rational thought) and a public position (versus a private life). In other words, our view of leadership is far too narrow. There is no single mold for notable leadership, only great leaders. And men in different spheres lead in different ways.

As Terry Glaspey has pointed out, Lewis should be counted a world-class leader because his ideas continue to shape our thought and culture.

When we think of leaders, we usually think of those who blaze new political trails, those who by their actions and their rhetoric draw masses of people to a new vision of society, or who make radical innovations that bring new security or strength to a people. To include Lewis in a series of books on great leaders might therefore seem, at first blush, an unusual choice. He never sought for or held any political office and made very few explicit public statements about political policy. His public speaking, though effective, was not extensive. But Lewis truly was a leader in the sphere of culture. He shaped the thoughts, and thereby the actions, of countless people in his own time and afterward, mostly through the quiet influence of his books.[347]

It is not surprising that Lewis affected the world through his books, since he was throughout his life enamored with reading and learning. His love for books began as a child. His parents were avid but eclectic readers and the interior of their home was overlaid with books. "There were books in the study, books in the drawing room, books in the cloakroom, books (two deep) in the great bookcase on the landing, books in a bedroom, books piled as high as my shoulder in the cistern attic, books of all kinds reflecting every transient stage of my parents' interest. . ."[348]

Equally important in Lewis' maturing love for literature was the influence of his teacher Kirkpatrick. While under his tutelage, Lewis studied the classics in the original. For instance, with the *Iliad* in one hand and a lexicon in the other, he would usually translate up to one hundred lines a day. He got so good at translating that he eventually was able to think in Greek. Of course he studied Virgil, Lucretius, Catullus, Tacitus, and Herodotus; as well as Cicero, Demosthenes, and the Greek dramatists. Lewis also learned French and read Voltaire, Stendhal, Balzac, and other works in French.[349]

During a typical school day Lewis had several hours for unsupervised reading. It was during these blissful afternoons that he poured over works by Boswell, Milton, Spencer, Shakespeare, Johnson, Andrew Lang, and William Morris; and he began to read medieval romances such as *Beowulf, Le Morte D'Arthur, Sir Gawain and the Green Knight,* and others. Providentially, his interest in romance literature led Lewis to pick up a copy of George MacDonald's *Phantastes,* a book that "baptized" his imagination and was ever so subtly the beginning of his conversion to Christianity.[350]

Books have always played a part in shaping leaders, and part of Lewis' unfolding influence as a cultural leader is due to the interest he inspired in classic literature—what he quaintly called "old books." In his well-known introduction to *The Incarnation of the Word of God* by Athanasius, Lewis suggests several reasons for reading older works. First, it is more enjoyable than wading through ponderous commentaries. Great books are "classic" precisely because they speak universally and directly to the average man. Secondly, the old books provide information with which to better judge and understand modern books. "A new book is still on its trial and the amateur is not in a position to judge it. It has to be tested against the great body of Christian thought down through the ages, and all its hidden implications (often unsuspected by the author himself) have to be brought to light."[351] In other words, the old books provide a standard of judgment.

Perhaps the principal reason for reading older books is that every age has its own bias, and the only we way we can escape the presuppositions of the present is by stepping into the past. Lewis put it in his usual winsome way:

Every age has its own outlook. It is specially good at seeing certain truths and specially liable to make certain mistakes. We all, therefore, need the books that will correct the characteristic mistakes of our own period. And that means the old books. . . Not, of course, that there is any magic about the past. People were no cleverer then than they are now; they make as many mistakes as we. But not the same mistakes. They will not flatter us in the errors we are already committing; and their own errors, being now open and palpable, will not endanger us. Two heads are better than one, not because either in infallible, but because they are unlikely to go wrong in the same direction. To be sure, the books of the future would be just as good a corrective as the books of the past, but unfortunately we cannot get at them.[352]

Every one would agree that a leader should be knowledgeable, especially in his own field; and to be so, he must read. Yet Lewis challenges leaders to take a step farther by taking a step backward. By reading older books—classics—the leader can free himself from a self-imposed provincialism of the mind. He can escape the mistakes of his rivals, challenge the assumptions of his age, and gain keener insight into contemporary problems. Instead of being a mere child of his times, he can become a mighty challenger of his age. And that is one of the earmarks of great leadership.

REASON

Theology means "the science of God," and I think any man who wants to think about God at all would like to have the clearest and most accurate ideas about Him which are available. You are not children: why should you be treated like children?[353]

When C.S. Lewis arrived in Bookham to begin studying with W.T. Kirkpatrick, he was expecting to meet a kindly old don—"dear Old Knock" his father called him. Instead he was confronted with an argumentative rationalist. In their very first conversation, as they traveled to Kirkpatrick's house, the young Lewis commented that the countryside was "wilder" than he expected. "Stop!" growled Kirkpatrick, as he pounced on the boy like a lion. "What do you mean by wildness and what grounds had you for not expecting it?" In short order Lewis was made to see his ignorance, that he "had no right to have any opinion whatever on the subject."[354]

Thus began some the happiest years of Lewis' life. Happy, because "Old Knock" not only guided young Jack into great literature, but also because he bequeathed to Lewis "a love of argument, intellectual disputation, the search for facts, and logical thinking."[355] In effect, Kirkpatrick taught Lewis to fully engage his mind in the pursuit of truth. Thus the crusty rationalist became father to the Christian apologist.

One key to the success of Lewis as a leading thinker in our age is his finely honed mind. Although he is frequently witty and imaginative, he is always logical. Indeed, it is fair to say that his reasonable righteousness made him appealing to both believers and doubters alike. To the faithful he provided assurances for their faith; to the unbeliever he gave arguments to believe. In both cases he extolled the virtue of reason.

Lewis held that his primary task as an apologist was to convince people that Christianity was true: not preferable but true; not enjoyable but true; not expedient but true. The central question about Christianity is simply this: Is it true? All other considerations are secondary, and in some cases, undermine the apologist's task. Speaking to a group of Anglican clergy and youth workers, Lewis reminded them, "The great difficulty is to get modern audiences to realize that you are preaching Christianity solely and simply because you happen to think it *true;* they always suppose you are preaching it because you like it or think it good for society or something of that sort."[356] In concluding this address, Lewis hammered home the chief point:

> *One of the great difficulties is to keep before the audience's mind the question of Truth. They always think you are recommending Christianity not because it is true but because it is good. And in the discussion they will at every moment try to escape from the issue "True—or False" into stuff about a good society, or morals or the incomes of Bishops, or the Spanish Inquisition, or France, or Poland—or anything whatever. You have to keep forcing them back, and again back, to the real point. . . One must keep on pointing out that Christianity is a statement which, if false, is of no importance, and, if true, of infinite importance.*[357]

Certain tendancies inherent in modern man's categories of thought make it difficult to convince him of Christianity's truth-claim. On the one hand, moderns tend to be pragmatic or practical.

> *Man is becoming as narrowly "practical" as the irrational animals. In lecturing to popular audiences I have repeatedly found it almost impossible to make them understand that I recommended Christianity because I thought its affirmations to be objectively true. They are simply not interested in the question of truth or falsehood. They only want to know if it will be comforting, or "inspiring," or socially useful.*[358]

On the other hand, modern man leans toward anti-rationalism or skepticism about reason itself. "Practicality, combined with vague notions of what Freud or Einstein said, has produced a general, and quite *unalarmed,* belief that reasoning proves nothing and that all thought is conditioned by irrational processes."[359]

In fine, Lewis rejected naturalism and its poison fruits, subjectivism and relativism, because it is self-contradictory.[360] In *Miracles,* he explains that naturalism views human thought, or reason, as a product of blind, irrational, natural forces. It is merely a biological by-product of millions of random natural occurrences. Therefore, reason is really based in irrational causes; and hence, "no thought is valid if it can be fully explained as the result of irrational causes."[361]

Yet naturalism insists that it is a correct or true theory of the universe while admitting it is based, like all human thought, on irrational causes. This is its undoing. As Lewis says:

> *A theory which explained everything else in the whole universe but which made it impossible to believe that our thinking was valid, would be utterly out of court. For that theory would itself have been reached by thinking, and if thinking is not valid that theory would, of course, be itself demolished. It would have destroyed its own credentials. It would be an argument which proved that no argument was sound—a proof that there are no such things as proofs—which is nonsense.*[362]

In 1941 Dr. James Welch, director of religious broadcasting for the BBC, asked Lewis to give a series of lectures over the radio. Believing that modern man was suffering from subjectivism and relativism, Lewis suggested a series on the objective basis of right and wrong. Entitled "Right and Wrong: A Clue to the Meaning of the Universe?" the lectures were a smashing success and were later put into print as *Mere Christianity.* One of the most famous examples of Lewis' razor-sharp reason (not to mention his delightful wit) occurred in these talks. Commenting on Augustine's argument that Christ, in claiming to be divine, was "either God or a bad man," Lewis said:

I am trying here to prevent anyone saying the really foolish thing that people often say about Him: "I'm ready to accept Jesus as a great moral teacher, but I don't accept His claim to be God." That is the one thing we must not say. A man who was merely a man and said the sort of things Jesus said would not be a great moral teacher. He would either be a lunatic—on a level with the man who says he is a poached egg—or else he would be the Devil of Hell. You must make your choice. Either this man was, and is, the Son of God: or else a madman or something worse. You can shut Him up for a fool, you can spit at Him and kill Him as a demon; or you can fall at His feet and call Him Lord and God. But let us not come with any patronizing nonsense about His being a great human teacher. He has not left that open to us. He did not intend to.[363]

Lewis was able to influence both his and future generations by the use of clear reasoning and solid argumentation. He did not manipulate or bully, as do some leaders. Rather, he respected the average man's intelligence and appealed to his reason. By doing so he won their allegiance. And any leader of sound mind can, and should, do the same.

MORALITY

Virtue is lovely, not merely obligatory; a celestial mistress, not a categorical imperative.[364]

*P*olitical leaders are fond of spouting platitudes about "traditional values" or "family values." Yet exactly what they mean by these terms is seldom clear; and most leaders are reluctant to give detailed explanations. Whose values are we talking about anyway? And do they have any basis in reality, or are they personal preferences? Why should I adopt a value that I find disagreeable to my "lifestyle?"

Lewis would give a simple (though not simplistic) and direct answer to these questions: There is only one moral code that has ever existed. It is universally binding on all peoples for all time. This code he called by different names: the moral law, the natural law, the law of practical reason, and even the Tao. Regardless of the name we might give it, there exists in the universe one moral standard that obliges all, and is written in the heart and mind of each.

The notion of natural law permeates Lewis' many works where it is discussed and defended in different contexts. For instance, when critiquing modern textbooks in *The Abolition of Man,* Lewis states:

> This thing which I have called for convenience the Tao, and
> which others may call Natural Law or Traditional Morality or
> the First Principles of Practical Reason or the First Platitudes,
> is not one among a series of possible systems of value. It is the sole
> source of all value judgements. If it is rejected, all value is rejected.
> If any value is retained, it is retained. The effort to refute it and
> raise a new system of value in its place is self-contradictory.
> There never has been, and never will be, a radically new judgement
> of value in the history of the world.[365]

In his essay, "The Poison of Subjectivism," he asserts:

> *This whole attempt to jettison traditional values as something*
> *subjective and to substitute a new scheme of values for them is*
> *wrong. It is like trying to lift yourself by your own coat collar. Let*
> *us get two propositions written into our minds with indelible ink.*
> *1) The human mind has no more power of inventing a new value*
> *than of planting a new sun in the sky or a new primary colour in*
> *the spectrum. 2) Every attempt to do so consists in arbitrarily*
> *selecting some one maxim of traditional morality, isolating it from*
> *the rest, and erecting it into an* unum necessarium.[366]

In his first BBC broadcasts, Lewis argued that everyone has an idea of "fair play." That is why we have disagreements about behavior and why we often rationalize, or excuse ourselves, when we violate the moral law. We assume that some ways of acting are proper and others are not.[367]

Lewis realized that not everyone would agree with him and that two main objections had to be overcome. The first is skepticism—the denial of the validity of reason. Yet Lewis refuted that objection, as we have seen, by demolishing its basis, Naturalism. The second objection is that "civilizations and different ages have had quite different moralities."[368] Lewis' answer?

> *The answer is that this is a lie—a good, solid, resounding lie.*
> *If a man will go into a library and spend a few days with the*
> Encyclopedia of Religion and Ethics *he will soon discover the*
> *massive unanimity of the practical reason in man. From the*
> *Babylonian* Hymn to Samos, *from the* Laws of Manu, *the* Book of
> the Dead, *the* Analects, *the Stoics, the Platonists, from Australian*
> *aborigines and Redskins, he will collect the same triumphantly*
> *monotonous denunciations of oppression, murder, treachery and*
> *falsehood, the same injunction of kindness to the aged, the young,*
> *and the weak, of almsgiving and impartiality and honesty.*[369]

This was not an idle challenge. Lewis himself did exactly as he dared others, and the result can be read in his book, *The Abolition of Man*. After his usual theoretical defense of the Moral Law, he provides an appendix with quotations from numerous ancient and modern sources from different cultures. And Lewis was right: there was, and is, general agreement on basic moral behavior.

Does that mean there are no moral differences? No. "There have been differences between their moralities, but these have never amounted to anything like a total difference."[370] The differences, in other words, are slight or perhaps refer to application—the agreement is broad and principial. For instance, "Men have differed as regards what people you ought to be unselfish to—whether it was only your own family, or your fellow countrymen, or everyone. But they have always agreed that you ought not to put yourself first. Selfishness has never been admired."[371]

It would be a mistake to assume that because Lewis repeatedly discussed the moral law, he was legalistic. He was not. The moral law was important to him because it provided "a clue to the meaning of the universe"—the subtitle of his original BBC broadcasts. If there is such a thing as a universal moral law then where did it come from? From Nature? No, because nature is irrational (according to the Naturalist) and provides no basis for thought, either theoretical or moral. From Society? No, for all societies basically agree on it. It must, Lewis concludes, come from God. Thus the Moral Law is for Lewis a strong argument for the existence of God.

This is not to say that his interest in morality was purely theoretical or apologetic. On the contrary, Lewis believed that faith in God and obedience to Him were paramount. But obedience was more than simply following a set a rules. God's goal is not to make us "nice men" but "new men;" who, by conforming to the moral law, are conformed to the image of His Son.

For mere improvement is not redemption, though redemption always improves people even here and now and will, in the end, improve then to a degree we cannot yet imagine. God became a man to turn creatures into sons: not simply to produce better men of the old kind but to produce a new kind of man.[372]

It is the "new man" who is distinctively equipped to be a leader. For being bound by the moral law and conformed to the image of Christ, he will lead by service and govern with virtue, the preeminent qualifications for leadership.

WINSTON CHURCHILL

(1874–1965)

Winston Churchill is unarguably the most famous leader of the twentieth century. Born in Blenheim Palace in 1874, he endured a difficult childhood, entered Sandhurst in 1893 and was commissioned as a lieutenant in 1895.

After a short military career, Churchill entered journalism, and while covering the Boer War, he was captured and imprisoned in Pretoria. After a miraculous escape, he returned to England a hero. His newfound fame then launched his political career. Over the span of nearly sixty years, Churchill's political star rose and fell many times. He held such high posts as Colonial Under-Secretary, Home Secretary, First Lord of the Admiralty, Chancellor of the Exchequer, and Prime Minister (twice). Yet because of his outspoken manner, and the fact that he had the audacity to switch parties twice, he was often isolated and distrusted by his colleagues, and was frequently out of office.

Churchill was also a voracious reader, prolific author, and persuasive communicator. Some of his better known books are historical works, The World Crisis *(5 Vols.) and* The Second World War *(6 Vols.),* Marlborough: His Life and Times *(6 Vols.) and* History of the English Speaking Peoples *(4 Vols.). Many of his speeches, which are excellent examples of his literary genius, have been published as* While England Slept, Blood, Sweat and Tears, The Unrelenting Struggle, *and* The End of the Beginning. *In addition, Churchill wrote numerous essays, character sketches, and his autobiography.*

A talented yet controversial figure throughout his life, Churchill's fame has come to rest on the courage and hope he inspired in the British people during the dark days of World War II when England was nearly defeated by the pagan forces of Hitler. Always the friend of freedom, Churchill refused to suffer surrender at the hand of a tyrant. His clarion call to "never give in" emboldened the British peoples to stave off defeat and made Churchill a symbol of hope to oppressed and freedom-loving peoples around the globe.

ENDURANCE

As I think most things are settled by destiny, when one has done one's best, the only thing is to await the result with patience.[373]

*P*atience is the passive counterpart of fortitude. Whereas fortitude is exercised in the active struggle with difficulties and dangers, patience is exercised in the resolute acceptance of what is hard to bear. It involves surrendering, not to circumstances, but to the will of God in the face of adversity. Its fruits are tranquillity of mind and determination of will. Patience is another word for endurance.

In some ways Churchill's life is a story of repeated and almost tragic adversity. Born to wealthy and famous parents, Churchill was neglected by his mother and cursed by his father. As his own son later wrote, "the neglect and lack of interest in him shown by his parents were remarkable, even judged by the standards of late Victorian and Edwardian days."[374] His lonely childhood was compounded by his sickly physique and maddening lisp, which made him the target of insults from schoolmates. Not surprisingly Churchill did poorly in school and thereafter suffered from a sense of intellectual inferiority.

Echoes of his father's criticism haunted Churchill throughout his tumultuous political life. Even before he left the Conservatives to join the Liberals in 1904, most Tories regarded Churchill with suspicion and distrust. Some of his colleagues used to jeer at him behind his back, deriding him as the "Blenheim Rat," while others ridiculed his lisp by hissing (thus showing their mastery of the letter "s") when he spoke in the House. This hostility toward Churchill is epitomized by Sir John Maxwell's note to a friend, "Winston Churchill is a _____ . I will leave you to fill in the blank, but use brown paint."[375]

As historian Martin Gilbert has noted:

His whole political career was an uphill struggle. Nor was it at all certain at any given moment of that struggle that he would

prevail. Throughout the forty years between his entering
Parliament and his becoming Prime Minister he suffered a
series of major setbacks. His footsteps were dogged by frequent
and strident accusations of past mistakes. His explanations were
mostly disbelieved, the evidence which he produced was ignored.
For those critics, and there were always many of them, who
wished to think that whatever Churchill touched he would
destroy, historical accuracy was of no importance.[376]

During World War I, for instance, Churchill was the First Lord of Admiralty. In that role he proposed that the Allies attack the Central Powers at the flank, and the site chosen was the Dardanelles. Although the plan was sound, the execution was boggled. The result was the death of more than 100,000 allied troops. Churchill was made the scapegoat and he was removed from his post.[377] For the rest of his life, Churchill's critics insisted that "he was reckless, even dangerous and perhaps unstable, and certainly lacking judgment."[378]

After the war, Churchill became Chancellor of the Exchequer, a position his father had once held. When he attempted to return England to the gold standard the British economy sank, strikes broke out in 1926 and unemployment skyrocketed. Again Churchill was blamed. In the election of 1929 he barely maintained a seat in Parliament, but was denied an influential place in the government. For the next ten years he was largely ignored and isolated. Many believed (and even hoped) that his career was over. When Lady Astor led a British delegation to Moscow, for instance, Stalin inquired of Churchill. Her reply was tart; "Churchill? Oh, he's finished."[379]

Lady Astor, of course, was wrong. With the onset of World War II, Churchill was again placed in the Admiralty and on May 8, 1940, he was appointed Prime Minister. The steely determination of Churchill's character, born of his adversity and criticism, served him well as a wartime leader. In his first address as Prime Minister to the House of Commons, he summoned his countrymen to endure any and all costs to achieve victory.

I would say to the House, as I said to those who have joined this
Government: "I have nothing to offer but blood, toil, tears and

sweat." We have before us an ordeal of the most grievous kind.
We have before us many, many long months of struggle and of
suffering. You ask, what is our policy? I will say; It is to wage
war, by sea, by land and air, with all our might and with all the
strength God can give us: to wage war against a monstrous
tyranny, never surpassed in the dark, lamentable catalogue of
human crime. That is our policy. You ask, What is our aim? I
can answer in one word: Victory—victory at all costs, victory
in spite of all terror, victory, however long and hard the road
may be; for without victory, there is no survival.[380]

By June of 1940, the British Force in Europe had been driven back to the
sea, and was rescued by a small armada of public and private vessels under
German bombardment. This "miracle of Dunkirk," as it was called, seemed to
many but the prelude to a German invasion of Britain itself. In his attempt to
rally the nation, Churchill repeated his willingness to endure the full fury of
the enemy yet not surrender.

Even though large tracts of Europe and many old and famous
States have fallen or may fall into the grip of the Gestapo and
all the odious apparatus of Nazi rule, we shall not flag or fail.
We shall go on to the end, we shall fight in France, we shall fight
on the seas and oceans, we shall fight with growing confidence
and growing strength in the air, we shall defend our island,
whatever the cost may be, we shall fight on the beaches, we shall
fight on the landing grounds, we shall fight in the fields and in the
streets, we shall fight in the hills; we shall never surrender. . .[381]

Churchill's political misfortunes—the constant criticism and years of
isolation—were only part of the adversity he endured. He was also accident
prone, for example, and when visiting New York he was run over by a taxi. His
recovery took more than a year. Also, Churchill was often vexed by serious
bouts of depression, what he called "my Black Dog."[382] Perhaps most painful
of all, his family proved to be a source of poignant sorrow. His youngest

daughter, Marigold, died at the age of two, and several of his adult children proved to be grave disappointments: Randolph became a violent drunk and Diana committed suicide a few years before Churchill's own death.

Churchill knew that criticism was the inevitable and unenviable lot of leaders, and that life—what he often called "destiny"—appoints to every man a portion of pain. That is reality, and leadership is all about knowing and facing the truth with courage. How did Churchill overcome repeated rejection and criticism and personal tragedy? He practiced the basic but difficult virtue of endurance. He simply made the decision early in life that, regardless of what trials he might face, he would never give in.

> *Never give in, never give in, never, never, never, never—in nothing, great or small, large or petty—never give in except to convictions of honor and good sense.*[383]

EXCELLENCE

We are all worms. But I intend to be a glowworm.[384]

L eadership is all about improvement and growth, about striving for excellence. Products must be improved, markets expanded, service enhanced. Policies must be refined and objectives clarified and well executed. The successful organization is marked by its growth toward excellence. And what applies to organizations equally applies to its leaders.

The problem, of course, is that leaders often lack either the humility or wisdom to see their faults; or if they do, they fail to summon the courage to admit them and change. It is easier to fix a system than a soul. Yet self-improvement, which requires looking squarely at one's weakness, is foundational to excellence. "Few men will admit their own failures; and even fewer will acknowledge that the true cause of failure lies within themselves," says Donald Krause. "But a person who practices self-discipline and continuously develops his level of skill seldom fails in the long run."[385]

Churchill's stature as a world-class leader is directly linked to his willingness to face his deficiencies and strive for self-improvement. Although he was often characterized as stubborn and arrogant, Churchill had a keen faculty for self-criticism. "Every night," he remarked to one of his aides, "I try myself by Court Martial to see if I have done anything effective during the day. I don't mean just pawing the ground, anyone can go through the motions, but something really effective."[386]

Self-criticism improved Churchill. He realized as a young man that if he were ever to become the leader he felt destined to be, he would have to devote himself to a plan of self-improvement. "Acutely aware of his deficiencies, he started to re-create himself in preparation for the life he wanted."[387] For instance, when he was stationed in India he came to recognize that due to his earlier stubbornness he was not intellectually prepared for leadership. Biographer Stephen Mansfield has accurately observed that this was a pivotal milestone in young Winston's life.

*India was an important transition for Churchill for reasons he
could not have foreseen. Here, for the first time, he came into
intimate contact with men of his own age who possessed a
university education. He marveled at their breadth of knowledge
and their ease of discourse on most any subject made him realize
how narrow his own education had been. When it came to history,
philosophy, law or theology, there were huge gaps in his
understanding. In an explosion of curiosity and ambition, he
began to devour books on his weakest subjects. With his mother
shipping him books as fast as she could, he gorged himself on some
of the greatest literature in the English language. This eager
pursuit of knowledge was a turning point in Churchill's life,
and the character he displayed in striving against his own
inadequacies undoubtedly marked the beginning of his manhood.*[388]

Recognizing his weakness, Churchill wrote, "I resolved to read history, philosophy, economics, and things like that. . ."[389] He thus embarked on a rigorous plan of self-education. He read Gibbon's eight-volume *Decline and Fall,* devoured the complete works of Macaulay, and plowed through Darwin, Aristotle, Plato, and Adam Smith. During the blazing Indian summer it was not uncommon for him to read four or five hours a day, pouring over such titles as Hallum's *Constitutional History,* Lecky's *European Morals,* or Pascal's *Provincial Letters.* In the words of his son, Churchill "thus became his own university."[390]

Churchill's self-education was more than a quest to satisfy his curiosity; it was a conscious effort to improve his skills and prepare himself for leadership. As he wrote his mother, "Macaulay, Gibbon, Plato, etc., must train the muscles to wield that sword to the greatest effect."[391] And wield a sword he did. It was said of him that before he entered a cabinet meeting he had already meticulously studied the subject at hand. He read every document he could find on the subject, assimilated the facts, and developed a plan.[392]

The journalist A. G. Gardiner, a contemporary of Churchill, once wrote an analysis in which he noted Churchill's "large mastery of ideas," his "power of statement," his "grasp of facts," and his "air of authority." How do we account for these "accomplishments" he asked? "It is not by application and industry alone that he has succeeded," Gardiner answered, "though he has these in an unusual degree. He labours at a subject with the doggedness of Stonewall Jackson. He polishes a speech as the lapidary polishes a stone. . . But more potent than his industry is his astonishing apprehension. . . Each task, however subversive of former tasks, finds him perfectly equipped, for he always knows his subject."[393]

Churchill also had other flaws to overcome in his quest for self-mastery and excellence. He saw, for instance, that a public leader must be an accomplished speaker. So he ceaselessly labored to correct his lisp and conquer his natural stage fright. And although he could never fully remove his embarrassing lisp, he nevertheless became the greatest orator of the twentieth century.

Whether he was expanding his knowledge or refining his oratory, Churchill was a man who strove for excellence. He believed in leadership by self-mastery rather than leadership by slick advertising. He knew that in the final analysis, the leader himself—his pride, his shallowness, his laziness, his stubbornness—is the greatest obstacle to his success. The man who faces his own flaws, and will strive to remove them, is prepared to lead with understanding and humility. If a leader is to inspire meaningful change, he must be willing to change himself. And the man who has mastered himself will earn the respect and loyalty of those who follow him.

HISTORY

*The greatest advances in human civilization have come when we recovered
what we had lost: when we learned the lessons of history.*[394]

One of the intangible qualities that set Churchill apart from other leaders
was his historical imagination. More than a simple knowledge of the
past, history was for Churchill a lens through which he viewed the world.
According to British historian Sir John H. Plumb, "History, for Churchill,
was not a subject like geography or mathematics, it was a part of his tempera-
ment, as much a part of his being as his social class and, indeed, closely allied
to it. . . it permeated everything which he touched, and it was the mainspring
of his politics and the secret of his immense mastery."[395] Churchill's historical
imagination was, claimed Isaiah Berlin, his "dominant category, the single,
central, organizing principle of his moral and intellectual universe. . ."[396]

Churchill's love of history began as a child. While bored with most
subjects, he excelled in this one. During his Harrow years, he literally
memorized twelve hundred lines of Macaulay's *Lays of Rome* and won a prize
for an impeccable recital. During his self-education program in India, he
studied history with such determination that years later he could still quote
from memory entire chapters of Gibbon and Macaulay.

How did Churchill's historical consciousness shape his career? Or to put
the question more generally, what is the relationship between historical
knowledge and leadership?

As noted earlier, history provides a leader with inspiration. This was
certainly true of Churchill, which was undoubtedly one reason he undertook
to write a lengthy biography of the Duke of Marlborough. Through his
historical studies Churchill came to the conclusion that great men, who rise to
the challenge of great events, shape history. "The fortunes of mankind in its
tremendous journeys are principally decided for good or ill. . . by its greatest
men and its greatest episodes."[397]

Churchill, of course, was challenged to become a great man who would
one day shape the history of his own generation. He learned from history to

believe in the invisible hand of destiny, and that he himself was destined to become a world-changing leader. For instance, when his political fortune was at a low point, he wrote to his wife, "My conviction that the greatest of my work is still to be done is strong within me and I ride reposefully along the gale."[398] And he was right. Then, when his conviction was vindicated by at last being installed as the Prime Minister during World War II, Churchill wrote, "I was conscious of a profound sense of relief. At last I had the authority to give directions over the whole scene. I felt as if I were walking with destiny, and that all my past life had been but a preparation for this hour and for this trial."[399]

Secondly, history provides a "perspective" for seeing both current and future events. Biographer Stephen Mansfield states the matter well.

> *Strong leaders throughout the centuries have learned to gain the "experience of age," and even of the ages, by learning what the past has to teach. History has the power to lift a leader out of the shortsightedness of his own times and give him the perspective of centuries. From this view, the problems of any one age seem less daunting and the real issues of man's existence gain focus. Instructed by his experience with the past, a leader can then throw open the windows of his age to what C.S. Lewis called "the clean sea-breeze of the centuries."[400]*

In other words, history is not so much about the past as it is about the present; for the two are intertwined with an invisible thread. The leader who knows the past is better equipped to confront current problems. History serves to make one a realist and, in the case of Churchill, made him a practical and shrewd politician. He understood that history is a multi-colored canvas, not a black and white sketch.

> *The world, nature, human beings, do not move like machines. The edges are never clear-cut, but always frayed. Nature never draws a line without smudging it. Conditions are so variable, episodes so unexpected, experiences so conflicting, that flexibility*

of judgment and a willingness to assume a somewhat humbler
attitude towards external phenomena may well play their
part in the equipment of a modern prime minister.[401]

A "humbler attitude" meant that Churchill was a cautious and prudent politician, especially when faced with war. "We realize that success cannot be guaranteed. There are no safe battles."[402]

When in the midst of battle, however, history again served him well. For example, Churchill was a great innovator during wartime. He reorganized the Navy and was the driving force behind the development of the armored tank. Derided as "Winston's Folly," Churchill's attempts to develop the tank as a solution to trench warfare were met with bureaucratic skepticism and apathy. Once designed and employed, however, it proved to be a decisive tactical advantage. Yet the inspiration for the tank came from Churchill's historical storehouse. "Remember the elephants of Roman times," he wrote in a letter. "These are mechanical elephants to break wire and earth-work phalanges."[403]

Moreover, history inspired Churchill to fight for all that was good and glorious in the tradition of Britain and the Christian West. He forgot himself (or at least saw himself as the embodiment of tradition) and felt called to live and die for the survival of Western civilization. As he said to the House of Commons on June 18, 1940, "I expect the Battle of Britain is about to begin. Upon this battle depends the survival of Christian civilization. Upon it depends our own British life, and the long continuity of our institutions and our Empire."[404]

Lastly, instead of being tied to the past, Churchill's historical imagination made him a far-seeing visionary. "The farther backward you can look," he once said, "the farther forward you can see."[405] Thus history is a key ingredient in shaping a leader's vision. Churchill, of course, projected a compelling vision— a vision that inspired both Britain and freedom fighters every where to resist the encroaching tyrannies of Nazism, Fascism, and Socialism. Live in light of the future and fight in light of history, for history will one day rise to judge us. "Think what your actions now will mean, years hence, when you remember them again. What kind of person will you wish you had been, what kind of sacrifices will you wish you had made, when you or those who survive you look back upon this from the future."[406]

History, then, galvanized Churchill to become a great leader, a prudent politician, and a visionary statesman. He walked in the twilight of the past and lived in the dawn of the future. And a leader who learns the lessons of history will be entrusted by destiny to shape the future. However, those who condemn the past are, as Churchill warned, in danger of being condemned by it, "If the present tries to sit in judgment of the past, it will lose the future."[407] Indeed, this is a sober warning for all who aspire to world-class leadership.

THE LESSONS OF LEADERSHIP

The true profit of virtuous deeds lies in the doing, and there is no fitting reward for the virtues apart from the virtues themselves and the graciousness of providence.[408]

The consciousness of a well-spent life and the recollection of many virtuous actions are exceedingly delightful.[409]

No man can become venerable but by virtue, or contemptible but by wickedness.[410]

This I regard as history's highest function, to let no worthy action be uncommemorated, and to hold out the reprobation of posterity as a terror to evil words and deeds.[411]

THE LESSONS OF LEADERSHIP

✠ A leader's faith is the invisible spring to his visible accomplishments; as a man thinks in his heart, so is he.

✠ The recognition of God's providential calling inspires a leader to overcome obstacles in order to fulfill his destiny.

✠ A leader's vision guides him where others have only dreamt of going.

✠ The key to successful communication is truth and conviction.

✠ Power is a sacred trust. How a leader uses his power reveals his true character.

✠ A wise leader will build on the foundation he inherited from the past, thereby leaving a legacy for the future.

✠ A leader knows that every great accomplishment takes time; therefore, he will persevere to the end of the goal.

✠ A leader often achieves more through his friends and associates than he could by himself. No man is an island.

✠ A genuine leader, as opposed to a charlatan, cares more about people than causes.

✠ The acceptance of duty causes a leader to lay aside self-interest for the good of others.

✠ The man who cannot govern himself is not fit to govern others.

✠ Christian spirituality refines a leader's character and enhances his ability to lead.

✠ No amount of talent ever replaces the need for old-fashioned industry. A leader works when others play.

✠ A key ingredient to great leadership is the ability to inspire hope.

✠ A leader's vision and optimism must be tempered by realism; otherwise, he will become a fanatic.

- A leader must practice what he preaches; he must back his words with deeds.

- A strict adherence to the principles of justice validates a leader's position and enhances his authority.

- It is better for a leader to fail courageously than to fail timidly. Cowardice is the death of leadership.

- A comprehensive world-view ennobles a leader's vision, lifting it out of the mundane and ordinary.

- A principled leader will adhere to his convictions regardless of the cost.

- Criticism is one of the inevitable tests of leadership. A great leader will respond to it with humility and will never resort to slander.

- A leader's sense of humor demonstrates his keen insight into human nature and his concern for his fellow man.

- A leader's humility causes him to sacrifice his reputation, if necessary, for the cause of truth and righteousness.

- Patriotic leadership means more than loving one's country. It may mean opposing one's country in order to make it right.

- The desire to learn and the influence of books play a large part in shaping a leader. He must be more knowledgeable than his followers.

- A leader can be more persuasive by reasoned arguments than by authoritative declamations.

- A leader influences the moral character of his followers; therefore he must have a clear idea of right and wrong.

- Leadership requires a hearty dose of fortitude—a leader must be able to endure criticism, disappointment, and conflict. He refuses to give in.

- A great leader continually strives for excellence. He believes in leadership by self-mastery not by self-promotion.

- Visionary leadership is rooted in a sense of history. Every great leader looks backward that he might see forward.

BIBLIOGRAPHY

Books

Anon. *Thoughts on Success*. Chicago: Triumph Books, 1995.

_____. *Thoughts on Leadership*. Chicago: Triumph Books, 1995.

Aquinas, Thomas. *The Summa Theologica, 2 Vols*. Vols. XIX and XX of Great Books ed. Chicago: Encyclopedia Britannica, 1952.

Arnold, S. G. *The Life of Patrick Henry of Virginia*. New York: Hurst and Company, 1845.

Barton, David. *Keys to Good Government According to the Founding Fathers*. Aledo, TX: WallBuilders Press, 1994.

Bennis, Warren and Burt Nanus. *Leaders: The Strategies For Taking Charge*. New York: Harper and Row, 1985.

Billingsley, Lloyd. *The Generation That Knew Not Josef: A Critique of Marxism and the Religious Left*. Portland, OR: Multnomah Press, 1985.

Blankenhorn, David. *Fatherless America: Confronting Our Most Urgent Social Problem*. New York: Basic Books, 1995.

Boorstin, Daniel J. *The Discoverers*. New York: Random House, 1983.

Burns, James MacGregor. *Leadership*. New York: Harper Torchbooks, 1978.

Bush, Douglas, ed. *The Portable Milton*. New York: Penguin Books, 1949.

Carson, Jane. *Patrick Henry, Prophet of the Revolution*. Brookneal, VA: Patrick Henry Memorial Foundation, 1992.

Chessman, G. Wallace. *Theodore Roosevelt and the Politics of Power*. Boston: Little, Brown and Company, 1969.

Chesterton, G. K. *Autobiography*. New York: Sheed and Ward, 1936.

_____. *Fancies Versus Fads*. London: Methuen and Company Ltd., 1927.

_____. *Orthodoxy*. New York: Dodd, Mead and Company, 1940.

_____. *The Uses of Diversity: A Book of Essays*. London: Methuen and Company Ltd., 1921.

_____. *What's Wrong With The World*. London: Cassell and Company Ltd., 1912.

Cicero. *The Letters and Treatises of Cicero and Pliny.* Vol. IX of The Harvard Classics ed. New York: P.F. Collier and Son Corporation, 1959.

Clemens, John K. and Steve Albrecht. *The Timeless Leader.* Holbrook, MA: Adams Media Corporation, 1995.

Clinton, Dr. Robert J. *The Making of a Leader.* Colorado Springs: NavPress, 1988.

Copeland, Lewis, ed. *The World's Great Speeches.* New York: The Book League of America, 1942.

Costigan, Giovanni. *Makers of Modern England: The Force of Individual Genius in History.* New York: Macmillan Company, 1967.

Covey, Stephen R. *Principle-Centered Leadership.* New York: Summit Books, 1990.

Daily, Patrick. *Patrick Henry—The Last Years—1789–1799.* Bedford, VA: Patrick Henry Memorial Foundation, 1986.

Dale, Alzina Stone. *The Outline of Sanity: A Biography of G. K. Chesterton.* Grand Rapids: William B. Eerdmans Publishing Company, 1982.

Dante, *Inferno,* trans. Charles Eliot Norton Vol. XXI of Great Books ed. Chicago: Encyclopedia Britannica, 1952.

Davies, Donald, ed. *The New Oxford Book of Christian Verse.* New York: Oxford University Press, 1981.

Eidsmoe, John. *Columbus and Cortez, Conquerors For Christ.* Green Forest, AR: New Leaf Press, 1992.

Eliot, Charles W. ed. *American Historical Documents, 1000–1904.* Vol. XLIII of The Harvard Classics. New York: P. F. Collier, 1959.

Eliott, Jonathan, ed. *The Debates in the Several State Conventions, on the Adoption of the Federal Constitution.* Philadelphia: n.p., 1907.

Elson, James M., ed. *Patrick Henry Essays: In Celebration of the Fiftieth Anniversary of the Patrick Henry Memorial Foundation.* Brookneal, VA: Patrick Henry Memorial Foundation, 1994.

Engstrom, Ted W. *The Making of a Christian Leader.* Grand Rapids: Zondervan Publishing House, 1976.

Freeman, Douglas Southall. *Lee.* (An abridgment in one volume). New York: Charles Scribner's Sons, 1961.

_____. *R.E. Lee,* 4 Vols. New York: Charles Scribner's Sons, 1947.

Gilbert, Martin, ed. *Churchill.* (Great Lives Observed). Englewood Cliffs: Prentice-Hall, Inc., 1967.

Glaspey, Terry W. *Not a Tame Lion: The Spiritual Legacy of C.S. Lewis.* Elkton, MD: Highland Books, 1996.

Grant, George. *Carry a Big Stick: The Uncommon Heroism of Theodore Roosevelt.* Elkton, MD: Highland Books, 1996.

_____. *Killer Angel: A Biography of Planned Parenthood's Founder Margaret Sanger.* New York: Ars Vitae Press and The Reformer Library, 1995.

_____. *The Changing of the Guard: The Vital Role Christians Must Play in America's Unfolding Political and Cultural Drama.* Nashville: Broadman and Holman Publishers, 1995.

_____. *The Last Crusader: The Untold Story of Christopher Columbus.* Wheaton, IL: Crossway Books, 1992.

_____. *The Patriot's Handbook.* Elkton, MD: Highland Books, 1996.

Grantham, Dewey W., ed. *Theodore Roosevelt.* (Great Lives Observed). Englewood Cliffs: Prentice Hall, Inc., 1971.

Green, Roger Lancelyn and Walter Hooper. *C.S. Lewis: A Biography.* New York: Harcourt Brace Jovanovich, 1974.

Greenleaf, Robert K. *Servant Leadership: A Journey into the Nature of Legitimate Power and Greatness.* New York: Paulist Press, 1977.

Hagedorn, Hermann. *Roosevelt in the Bad Lands.* Boston: Houghton Mifflin Company, 1921.

Hall, David W. *The Arrogance of the Modern: Historical Theology Held in Contempt.* Oak Ridge, TN: The Calvin Institute, 1997.

Hamilton, Alexander, James Madison, and John Jay. *The Federalist.* Vol. XLIII of Great Books ed. Chicago: Encyclopedia Britannica, 1952.

Hardwick, Kevin R. *Patrick Henry: Economic, Domestic and Political Life in Eighteenth-Century Virginia.* Brookneal, VA: Patrick Henry Memorial Foundation, 1991.

Hayward, Steven F. *Churchill On Leadership: Executive Success in the Face of Adversity.* Rocklin, CA: Prima Publishing, 1997.

Henry, William Wirt. *Patrick Henry: Life, Correspondence and Speeches,* 3 Vols. Harrisonburg, VA: Sprinkle Publications, 1993 [1891].

Himmelfarb, Gertrude. *On Looking Into the Abyss: Untimely Thoughts on Culture and Society*. New York: Vintage Books, 1994.

_____. *The Demoralization of Society: From Victorian Virtues to Modern Values*. New York: Vintage Books, 1994.

Hower, Stephen D. *Sharpening the Sword: A Call to Strong and Courageous Leadership*. Saint Louis: Concordia Publishing House, 1996.

Jane, Cecil, tr. *The Journal of Christopher Columbus*. New York: Bramhall House, 1960.

Johnson, Samuel. *Selected Writings*. London: Penguin Books, 1968.

Jones, J. William. *Life and Letters of Robert Edward Lee, Soldier and Man*. Harrisonburg, VA: Sprinkle Publications, 1978 [1909].

Kirk, Russell. *Redeeming the Time*. Wilmington, DE: Intercollegiate Studies Institute, 1996.

_____. *The Conservative Mind: From Burke to Eliot*. Washington, DC: Regnery Publishing, Inc., 1985.

_____. *The Portable Conservative Reader*. New York: Penguin Books, 1982.

Krause, Donald G. *The Way of the Leader*. New York: The Berkeley Publishing Group, 1997.

Kreeft, Peter. *A Shorter Summa: The Most Essential Philosophical Passages of St. Thomas Aquinas' Summa Theologica*. San Francisco: Ignatius Press, 1993.

Kuyper, Abraham. *Christianity: A Total World and Life System*. (An abridged edition of the 1898 Stone Lectures on Calvinism). Marlborough, NH: Plymouth Rock Foundation, 1996.

Langely, McKendree R. *The Practice of Political Spirituality: Episodes from the Public Career of Abraham Kuyper, 1879–1918*. Ontario: Paideia Press, 1984.

Lasch, Christopher. *Haven in a Heartless World: The Family Besieged*. New York: Basic Books, Inc., Publishers, 1977.

Lean, Garth. *God's Politician: William Wilberforce's Struggle*. Colorado Springs: Helmers and Howard, 1987.

Lee, Harris W. *Effective Church Leadership: A Practical Sourcebook*. Minneapolis: Augsburg, 1989.

Lewis, C.S. *The Abolition of Man*. London: Geoffrey Bles, 1962.

_____. *Christian Reflections*. London: Geoffrey Bles, 1967.

_____. *God In the Dock: Essays on Theology and Ethics*. Grand Rapids: William B. Eerdmans, 1970.

_____. *Mere Christianity*. London: Geoffrey Bles, 1953.

_____. *Miracles: A Preliminary Study*. London: Geoffrey Bles, 1947.

_____. *Present Concerns*. San Diego: Harcourt Brace Jovanovich, 1986.

Lindskoog, Kathryn. *C.S. Lewis: Mere Christian*. Downers Grove: Intervarsity Press, 1981.

Mansfield, Stephen. *Never Give In: The Extraordinary Character of Winston Churchill*. Elkton, MD: Highland Books, 1995.

Manz, Charles C. and Henry P. Sims, Jr. *Super Leadership: Leading Others to Lead Themselves*. New York: Prentice Hall Press, 1989.

Marshall, John. *The Life of Washington,* 4 Vols. The Citizens' Guild of Washington's Boyhood Home, Fredericksburg, VA. 1926.

Marshall, Peter and David Manuel. *The Light and the Glory*. Grand Rapids: Fleming H. Revell, 1977.

Mathews, Basil. *Booker T. Washington, Educator and Interracial Interpreter*. London: SCM Press Ltd., 1949.

Maxwell, John C. *Developing the Leader Within You*. Nashville: Thomas Nelson Publishers, 1993.

McCants, David. *Patrick Henry: The Orator*. New York: Greenwood Press, 1990.

Meade, Robert D. *Patrick Henry: Patriot in the Making*. Philadelphia: J.B. Lippincott, 1957.

Millard, Catherine. *Great American Statesmen and Heroes*. Camp Hill, PA: Horizon Books, 1995.

_____. *The Rewriting of America's History*. Camp Hill, PA: Horizon Books, 1991.

Miller, Calvin. *The Empowered Leader: 10 Keys to Servant Leadership*. Nashville: Broadman and Holman Publishers, 1995.

Miller, Nathan. *Theodore Roosevelt: A Life*. New York: William Morrow, 1992.

Morgan, George. *The True Patrick Henry*. Philadelphia: J.B. Lippincott Company, 1929 [1907].

Morison, Samuel Eliot. *Admiral of the Ocean Sea*. New York: Time Incorporated, 1962.

Page, Thomas Nelson. *Robert E. Lee: Man and Soldier,* 2 Vols. New York: Charles Scribner's Sons, 1912.

Payne, Leanne. *Crisis In Masculinity*. Wheaton, IL: Crossway Books, 1985.

Pearson, John. *The Private Lives of Winston Churchill*. New York: Simon and Schuster, 1991.

Peters, Thomas C. *Battling for the Modern Mind: A Beginner's Chesterton*. Saint Louis, MO: Concordia Publishing House, 1994.

Plutarch. *The Lives of the Noble Grecians and Romans*. Vol. XIV of Great Books ed., Chicago: Encyclopedia Britannica, Inc., 1952.

Pollock, John. *Wilberforce*. New York: St. Martin's Press, 1977.

Praamsma, L. *Let Christ Be King: Reflections on the Life and Times of Abraham Kuyper*. Ontario: Paideia Press, 1978.

Pringle, Henry F. *Theodore Roosevelt*. New York: Konecky and Konecky, 1931.

Roche, George. *A World Without Heroes: The Modern Tragedy*. Hillsdale, MI: Hillsdale College Press, 1987.

Roosevelt, Theodore. *An Autobiography*. New York: Charles Scribner's Sons, 1925.

_____. *Foes of Our Own Household*. New York: Scribners, 1926.

Ross, James Bruce and Mary Martin McLaughlin, eds. *The Portable Renaissance Reader*. New York: Penguin Books, 1981.

_____. *The Portable Medieval Reader*. New York: Penguin Books, 1977 [1949].

Sanders, J. Oswald. *Spiritual Leadership*. Chicago: Moody Press, 1967.

Sayer, George. *Jack: A Life of C.S. Lewis*. Wheaton, IL: Crossway Books, 1994.

Shakespeare, William. *The Portable Shakespeare*. New York: Penguin Books, 1944.

Spencer, Samuel R. Jr. *Booker T. Washington and the Negro's Place in American Life*. Boston: Little, Brown and Company, 1955.

Tacitus. *The Annuals*. Vol. XV of Great Books ed. Chicago: Encyclopedia Britannica, 1952.

Taylor, Robert Lewis. *Winston Churchill: An Internal Study of Greatness*. Garden City, NY: Doubleday and Company, 1952.

Thomas, Emory M. Robert E. *Lee: A Biography*. New York: WW Norton and Company, 1995.

Thornbrough, Emma Lou. *Booker T. Washington*. (Great Lives Observed). New Jersey: Prentice-Hall, Inc., 1969.

Vanden Berg, Frank. *Abraham Kuyper: A Biography*. Ontario: Paideia Press, 1978.

Vaughan, David J. *Give Me Liberty: The Uncompromising Statesmanship of Patrick Henry*. Elkton, MD: Highland Books, 1997.

Wagenknecht, Edward. *The Seven Worlds of Theodore Roosevelt*. New York: Longmans and Green, 1958.

Ward, Masie. *Gilbert Keith Chesterton*. New York: Sheed and Ward, 1943.
_____. *Return to Chesterton*. New York: Sheed and Ward, 1952.

Warner, Oliver. *William Wilberforce and His Times*. New York: Arco Publishing Company, Inc., 1963.

Washington, Booker T. *Up From Slavery*. New York: Dover Publications, Inc., 1995 [1901].

Wilberforce, William. *A Practical View of the Prevailing Religious System of Professed Christians, in the Higher and Middle Classes, Contrasted With Real Christianity*. Vol. II. of The Evangelical Family Library. New York: American Tract Society, nd.

Wilkins, J. Stephen. *Call of Duty: The Sterling Nobility of Robert E. Lee*. Elkton, MD: Highland Books, 1997.

Wills, Gary. *Chesterton: Man and Mask*. New York: Sheed and Ward, 1961.

Reference Works

A Lions Handbook: The History of Christianity. Tim Dowley, ed. Oxford: Lion Publishing, 1977.

American Reformers. Alden Whitman, ed. New York: The H. W. Wilson Company, 1985.

Cambridge Biographical Dictionary. Magnus Magnusson, ed. Cambridge: Cambridge University Press, 1990.

Chambers Biographical Dictionary. J. O. Thorne and T. C. Collocott, eds. Edinburgh: W & R Chambers Ltd., 1984.

Dictionary of American Biography. Allen Johnson, ed. New York: Charles Scribner's Sons, 1957 [1907].

Evangelical Dictionary of Theology. Walter A. E. Elwell, ed. Grand Rapids: Baker Book House, 1984.

Great Events From History II: Human Rights Series. Vol. I. 1900–1936. Frank N. Magill, ed. Pasadena: Salem Press, 1992.

Great Events From History: Modern European Series. Frank N. Magill, ed. Englewood Cliffs: Salem Press, 1973.

Great Lives From History: American Series. Frank N. Magill, ed. Pasadena: Salem Press, 1987.

New 20th Century Encyclopedia of Religious Knowledge. J. D. Douglas, ed. Grand Rapids: Baker Book House, 1991.

The Dictionary of National Biography (1931–1940). L. G. Wickham Legg, ed. Oxford: Oxford University Press, 1950.

The Dictionary of National Biography (1961–1970). E. T. Williams, C. S. Nicholls, eds. Oxford: Oxford University Press, 1981.

The Dictionary of National Biography (Vol. XXI). Sir Leslie Stephen and Sir Sidney Lee, eds. Oxford: Oxford University Press, 1959–1969 [1917].

The Little Oxford Dictionary of Quotations. Susan Ratcliffe, ed. New York: Oxford University Press, 1994.

The New International Dictionary of the Christian Church. J. D. Douglas, ed. Grand Rapids: Zondervan, 1978.

Who's Who in Christian History. J. D. Douglas, ed. Wheaton, IL: Tyndale House Publishers, Inc., 1992.

Who's Who in History, Vol. II. England. C. R. W. Routh, ed. Oxford: Blackwell, 1964.

Magazines

Christian History, Vol. IV, No. 3.
Christian History, Vol. XVI, No. 1.
Christianity Today, September, 1985.
Credenda Agenda, Vol. 9, No. 2.

ENDNOTES

1. Warren Bennis and Burt Nanus, *Leaders: Strategies For Taking Charge* (New York: Harper and Row, 1985), p. 20.
2. See Donald Krause, *The Way of the Leader* (New York: Berkeley Publishing Group, 1997), and John K. Clemens and Steve Albrecht, *The Timeless Leader* (Holbrook, MA: Adams Media corporation, 1995).
3. A notable exception is J. Oswald Sanders, *Spiritual Leadership* (Chicago: Moody Press, 1967).
4. Quoted in Ted Engstrom, *The Making of a Christian Leader* (Grand Rapids: Zondervan Publishing House, 1976), p. 207.
5. George Roche, *A World Without Heroes: The Modern Tragedy* (Hillsdale, MI: Hillsdale College Press, 1987), p. 346.
6. Dante, *Inferno,* trans. Charles Eliot Norton (Vol. XXI of the Great Books ed., Chicago: Encyclopedia Britannica, 1952), Canto XXVI, Par. 112.
7. George Herbert in Donald Davie, ed., *The New Oxford Book of Christian Verse* (New York: Oxford University Press, 1981),p. 77.
8. Amiel in Roche, Op. Cit., p. viii.
9. Quoted in David J. Vaughan, *Give Me Liberty: The Uncompromising Statesmanship of Patrick Henry* (Elkton, MD: Highland Books, 1997), pp. 80–85.
10. Edmund Burke in Anon., *Thoughts on Leadership* (Chicago: Triumph Books, 1995), p. 14.
11. Robert J. Clinton, *The Making of a Leader* (Colorado Springs: NavPRess, 1988), p. 9.
12. Engstrom, Op. Cit., p. 11.
13. Ibid.
14. Bennis and Nanus, Op. Cit., p. 2.
15. Krause, Op. Cit., ix.
16. Ibid.
17. Leanne Payne, *Crisis In Masculinity* (Wheaton: Crossway Books, 1985), p. 14.
18. David Blankenhorn, *Fatherless America: Confronting Our Most Urgent Social Problem* (New York: Basic Books, 1995), p. 17.
19. Ibid.
20. Ibid., p. 4.
21. Ibid., p. 2.
22. Quoted in Roche, Op. Cit., p. 30.
23. Ibid., p. 353.
24. C.S. Lewis, *The Abolition of Man* (London: Geoffrey Bles, 1962), p. 21.
25. See Romans chapter one.
26. Quoted in *Thoughts on Leadership,* p. 145.
27. Lloyd Billingsley, *The Generation That Knew Not Josef: A Critique of Marxism and the Religious Left* (Portland, OR: Multnomah Press, 1985), pp. 34–35.
28. McCracken in *Thoughts on Leadership,* p. 51.
29. James MacGregor Burns, *Leadership* (New York: Harper Torchbooks, 1978), p. 446.
30. Quoted in Harris W. Lee, *Effective Church Leadership: A Practical Sourcebook* (Minneapolis: Augsburg, 1989), p. 12.

31. Krause, Op. Cit., p. xi.
32. John C. Maxwell, *Developing the Leader Within You* (Nashville: Thomas Nelson Publishers, 1993), p. 1.
33. Georges in Ibid.
34. Burns, Op. Cit., p. 418.
35. Engstrom, Op. Cit., p. 20.
36. Krause, Op. Cit., p. 3.
37. Clinton, Op. Cit., p. 14.
38. Albrecht and Clemens, Op. Cit., xviii.
39. Packard in *Thoughts on Leadership,* p. 101.
40. Truman in Ibid.
41. Burns, Op. Cit., p. 447.
42. Luke 12: 15
43. Calvin Miller, *The Empowered Leader: 10 Keys to Servant Leadership* (Nashville: Broadman and Holman Publishers, 1995), p. 121.
44. Quoted in Susan Ratcliffe, ed., *The Little Oxford Dictionary of Quotations* (New York: Oxford, 1994), p. 372.
45. Proverbs 4:23
46. C. Miller, Op. Cit., p. 117.
47. Alexander Hamilton, James Madison and John Jay, *The Federalist* (Vol. XLIII of Great Books ed. Chicago: Encyclopedia Britannica, 1952), #57, p. 176–177.
48. Jonathan Eliott, ed., *The Debates in the Several State Conventions, on the Adoption of the Federal Constitution* (Philadelphia, n.p., 1907), III, 536–537.
49. Gertrude Himmelfarb, *The Demoralization of Society: From Victorian Virtues to Modern Values* (New York: Vintage Books, 1994), p. 8.
50. Quoted in Russell Kirk, *Redeeming the Time* (Wilmington, DE: Intercollegiate Studies Institute, 1996), p. 55.
51. Peter Kreeft, *A Shorter Summa: The Most Essential Philosophical Passages of St. Thomas Aquinas' Summa Theologica* (San Francisco: Ignatius Press, 1993), pp. 155–156.
52. Thomas Aquinas, *The Summa Theologica,* 2 Vols. (Vol. XIX and XX of Great Books ed. Chicago: Encyclopedia Britannica, 1952), Part I-II, Q. 61. Art. 2.
53. "The Chivalric Ideal" in James Bruce Ross and Mary Martin McLaughlin, eds., *The Portable Medieval Reader* (New York: Penguin Books, 1977), pp. 91–92.
54. Dante, Op. Cit., Canto XXVI, Par. 112.
55. *Macbeth,* One: VII in *The Portable Shakespeare* (New York: Penguin Books, 1944), p. 147.
56. Douglas Bush, ed. *The Portable Milton* (New York: Penguin Books, 1949), p. 137.
57. Charles W. Eliot, ed., *American Historical Documents, 1000–1904.* Vol. XLIII of Harvard Classics ed. (New York: P.F. Collier and Son Corporation, 1959), pp. 242–243.
58. Kirk, *Redeeming the Time,* p. 55.
59. Quoted in Vaughan, Op. Cit., p. 221.
60. Maxwell, Op. Cit., p. 32.
61. Kirk, *Redeeming the Time,* p. 55.
62. Terry Glaspey, *Not a Tame Lion: The Spiritual Legacy of C.S. Lewis* (Elkton, MD: Highland Books, 1996), p. 172.
63. Himmelfarb, *The Demoralization of Society,* p. 10–11.
64. George Grant, *Killer Angel: A Biography of Planned Parenthood's Founder Margaret Sanger* (New York: Ars Vitae Press and The Reformer Library, 1995), p. 5.
65. Quoted in David Barton, *Keys to Good Government According to the Founding Fathers* (Aledo, TX: WallBuilders Press, 1994), p. 5.

66. Lewis, *The Abolition of Man,* p. 50.
67. Robert K. Greenleaf, *Servant Leadership: A Journey into the Nature of Legitimate Power and Greatness* (New York: Paulist Press, 1977), p. 16.
68. Quoted in Maxwell, Op. Cit., p. 34.
69. Quoted in Ibid.
70. In Ibid., p. 83.
71. See the qualifications for leadership in 1Tim. 3 and Titus 1.
72. George Grant, *Carry a Big Stick: The Uncommon Heroism of Theodore Roosevelt* (Elkton, MD: Highland Books, 1996), pp. 119–121.
73. Matt 20:25–28 KJV
74. Greenleaf, Op. Cit., p. 10.
75. George Grant, *The Changing of the Guard: The Vital Role Christians Must Play in America's Unfolding Political and Cultural Drama* (Nashville: Broadman and Holman Publisher, 1995), p. 165.
76. In Grant, *Carry a Big Stick,* p. 168.
77. C.S. Lewis in Glaspey, Op. Cit., p. 171.
78. See "Can Virtue Be Taught?" in Russell Kirk, *Redeeming the Time,* pp. 53–67.
79. Bennis and Nanus, Op. Cit., p. 223.
80. Kirk, *Redeeming the Time,* p. 60.
81. Christopher Lasch, *Haven in a Heartless World: The Family Besieged* (New York: Basic Books, Inc., Publishers, 1977), p. 3.
82. Ibid., p. 4.
83. G.K. Chesterton, *What's Wrong With the World* (London: Cassell and Company Ltd., 1912), p. 199.
84. Ibid., pp. 199–200.
85. Kirk, *Redeeming the Time,* p. 61.
86. I Tim. 3: 15; II Tim. 3: 15–16.
87. See Mt. 28:18–20.
88. Grant, *Changing of the Guard,* p. 169.
89. Kirk, *Redeeming the Time,* p. 62.
90. Bernard of Chartres in *Little Oxford Dictionary of Quotations,* p. 317.
91. David W. Hall, *The Arrogance of the Modern: Historical Theology Held in Contempt* (Oak Ridge, TN: The Calvin Institute, 1997), p. 5.
92. In Glaspey, Op. Cit., p. 155.
93. Plutarch, *The Lives of the Noble Grecians and Romans* (Vol. XIV of Great Books ed. Chicago: Encyclopedia Britannica, Inc., 1952), p. 121.
94. Ibid., p. 122.
95. Grant, *Carry a Big Stick,* p. 163.
96. Ibid., p. 206.
97. Quoted in Hall, Op. Cit., p. 97.
98. Gertrude Himmelfarb, *Looking Into the Abyss: Untimely Thoughts on Culture and Society* (New York: Vintage Books, 1994), p. 37.
99. Ibid., p. 36.
100. Ibid., p. 46.
101. Quoted in Grant, *Carry a Big Stick,* p. 89.
102. Hoge in Hall, Op. Cit., p. 12.
103. Roosevelt in Grant, *Carry a Big Stick,* p. 11.
104. Coolidge in Steven F. Hayward, *Churchill On Leadership: Executive Success in the Face of Adversity* (Rocklin, CA: Prima Publishing, 1997), xi.

105. John Marshall, *The Life of Washington,* 4 Vols. (The Citizens' Guild of Washington's Boyhood Home Fredericksburg, VA: 1926, [1804–1807]), Vol. I, ix.
106. Columbus in George Grant, *The Last Crusader: The Untold Story of Christopher Columbus* (Wheaton, IL: Crossway Books, 1992), p. 106.
107. John Eidsmoe, *Columbus and Cortez, Conquerors For Christ* (Green Forest, AR: New Leaf Press, 1992), chapters 1 and 4.
108. Grant, *The Last Crusader,* p. 85.
109. Ibid.
110. Peter Marshall and David Manuel, *The Light and the Glory* (Grand Rapids: Fleming H. Revell, 1977), p. 37.
111. Ibid., p. 38.
112. Grant, *The Last Crusader,* p. 25.
113. Marshall, *The Light and the Glory,* p. 41.
114. Grant, *The Last Crusader,* p. 21.
115. Pietro Martire D`Anghiera in James Bruce Ross and Mary Martin McLaughlin, eds., *The Portable Renaissance Reader* (New York: Penguin Books, 1981), p. 150.
116. Samuel Eliot Morison, *Admiral of the Ocean Sea* (New York: Time Incorporated, 1962), p. 41.
117. Ibid., p. 42.
118. Columbus in Catherine Millard, *Great American Statesmen and Heroes* (Camp Hill, PA: Horizon Books, 1995), p. 4.
119. I have merged the story from differing accounts in Morison, 7–8, and Marshall, 39.
120. Morison, Op. Cit., p. 8.
121. Ibid., p. 344.
122. Ibid., p. 42.
123. Daniel J. Boorstin, *The Discoverers* (New York: Random House, 1983), p. 238.
124. Columbus in Grant, *The Last Crusader,* p. 121.
125. Boorstin, Op. Cit., p. 231.
126. Ibid., p. 227.
127. Quoted in Grant, *The Last Crusader,* p. 139.
128. Ibid., pp. 95–96.
129. In Boorstin, Op. Cit., p. 230.
130. In Millard, *Great American Statesmen and Heroes,* p. 3.
131. Grant, *The Last Crusader,* p. 68.
132. Ibid., p. 67.
133. Ibid.
134. Marshall, Op. Cit., p. 65. Marshall and Manuel have given a distorted picture of Columbus' quest for gold, as if he were an erring prodigal. They show little ability to appreciate the Medieval worldview and how the Crusades fit into it.
135. Grant, *The Last Crusader,* p. 66.
136. Mt. 28: 19–20.
137. In Morison, Op. Cit., p. 271.
138. In Ibid., p. 536.
139. Ibid.
140. Liberty Speech in S.G. Arnold, *The Life of Patrick Henry of Virginia* (New York: Hurst and Company, 1845), p. 107 ff.
141. Quoted in David McCants, *Patrick Henry: The Orator* (New York: Greenwood Press, 1990), p. 7.
142. Quoted in Jane Carson, *Patrick Henry, Prophet of the Revolution* (Brookneal, VA: Patrick Henry Memorial Foundation, 1992), p. 2.

143. In William Wirt Henry, *Patrick Henry: Life, Correspondence and Speeches,* 3 Vols. (Harrisonburg, VA: Sprinkle Publications), Vol. II, p. 493.
144. Ibid.,p. 488.
145. In James M. Elson, "Patrick Henry, Orator," in *Patrick Henry Essays: In Celebration of the Fiftieth Anniversary of the Patrick Henry Memorial Foundation* (Brookneal, VA: Patrick Henry Memorial Foundation, 1994), p. 15.
146. Robert D. Meade, *Patriot in the Making* (Philadelphia: J.B. Lipponcott, 1957), p. 71.
147. WW Henry, Op. Cit., Vol. II, p. 248; Meade, Op. Cit., Vol. I, p. 55.
148. In WW Henry, Op. Cit., Vol. I, pp. 267–268.
149. Alexander in WW Henry, Op. Cit., Vol. II, p. 500.
150. Patrick Henry, Ratification Speech in Ibid., Vol. III.
151. Patrick Daily, *Patrick Henry—The Last Years—1789–1799* (Bedford, VA: Patrick Henry Memorial Foundation, 1986), p. 41.
152. WW Henry, Op. Cit., Vol. II, p. 184.
153. Washington in ibid., p. 432.
154. Blair in Ibid., Vol. II, p. 595.
155. Anonymous author in George Morgan, *The True Patrick Henry* (Philadelphia: J.B. Lippincott Company, 1929), p. 136.
156. Henry in Ratification Speech.
157. Kevin R. Hardwick, *Patrick Henry: Economic, Domestic and Political Life in Eighteenth - Century Virginia* (Brookneal, VA: Patrick Henry Memorial Foundation), pp. 26–27.
158. Russell Kirk, *The Conservative Mind: From Burke to Eliot* (Washington, DC: Regnery Publishing, Inc., 1985), 8–9; *The Portable Conservative Reader,* (New York: Penguin Books, 1982), xv-xxi.
159. Kirk, *The Portable Conservative Reader,* xvi.
160. Ibid., xvii.
161. Henry in Ratification Speech.
162. WW Henry, 2.522–525.
163. Kirk, *The Portable Conservative Reader,* xx.
164. Wilberforce in Garth Lean, *God's Politician: William Wilberforce's Struggle* (Colorado Springs: Helmers and Howard, 1987), p. 47.
165. Quoted in Engstrom, Op. Cit., p. 208.
166. John Pollock, *Wilberforce* (New York: St. Martin's Press, 1977), pp. 49 ff.
167. *Christian History,* Vol. XVI, No. 1, p. 17.
168. Lean, Op. Cit., p. 54.
169. Ibid., p. 65.
170. Ibid., p. 64.
171. Oliver Warner, *William Wilberforce and His Times* (New York: Arco Publishing Company, Inc., 1963), p. 103.
172. Lean, Op. Cit., p. 106.
173. Ibid., p. 112.
174. *Christian History,* Vol. XVI, No. 1, p. 24.
175. Ibid., pp. 53, 25–26.
176. Ibid.
177. William Wilberforce, *A Practical View of the Prevailing Religious System of Professed Christians, in the Higher and Middle Classes, Contrasted With Real Christianity. Vol. II of the Evangelical Family Library* (New York: American Tract Society, n.d.), p. 259.
178. Quoted in Lean, Op. Cit., p. 74.
179. Ibid.
180. Ibid., p. 85.

181. Ibid., p. 105.
182. Ibid., p. 70.
183. Gal. 5: 6.
184. Robert E. Lee in J. Stephen Wilkins, *Call of Duty: The Sterling Nobility of Robert E. Lee* (Elkton, MD: Highland Books, 1997), p. 226.
185. Ibid.
186. Ibid., p. 42.
187. Ibid., p. 212.
188. Ibid., p. 88.
189. Douglas Southall Freeman, *Lee* (An abridgment in one volume). (New York: Charles Scribner's Sons, 1961), p. 587.
190. Wilkins, Op. Cit., p. 229.
191. Ibid., p. 233.
192. Thomas Nelson Page, *Robert E. Lee: Man and Soldier,* 2 Vols. (New York: Charles Scribner's Sons, 1912), Vol. II, p. 349.
193. Quoted in Wilkins, Op. Cit., p. 227.
194. Ibid., p. 160.
195. Freeman (abridgment), p. 587.
196. Lee quoted in Wilkins, Op. Cit., p. 249.
197. Freeman (abridgment), p. 5.
198. Ibid., p. 8.
199. Ibid., p. 10.
200. Wilkins, Op. Cit., p. 59.
201. Ibid., p. 254.
202. Douglas Freeman, *R.E. Lee,* 4 Vols. (New York: Charles Scribner's Sons, 1947), Vol. III, p. 528.
203. Wilkins, Op. Cit., p. 238.
204. Freeman, Vol. IV, p. 505.
205. Lee quoted in Wilkins, Op. Cit., p. 187.
206. Freeman (abridgment). Pp. 582–583.
207. Ibid., p. 586.
208. Emory M. Thomas, *Robert E. Lee: A Biography* (New York: W.W. Norton and Company, 1995), pp. 45–46.
209. Wilkins, Op. Cit., p. 120.
210. Ibid., p. 188.
211. J. William Jones, *Life and Letters of Robert Edward Lee, Soldier and Man* (Harrisonburg, VA: Sprinkle Publications, 1978 [1909]), p. 467.
212. Wilkins, Op. Cit., p. 189.
213. Ibid., p. 191.
214. Freeman, Vol. IX, p. 298.
215. Wilkins, Op. Cit., p. 191.
216. Ibid., pp. 309–310.
217. Ibid., p. 232.
218. Freeman, Vol. IV, p. 504.
219. Quoted in Catherine Millard, *The Rewriting of America's History* (Camp Hill, PA: Horizon Books, 1991), p. 186.
220. Booker T. Washington, *Up From Slavery* (New York: Dover Publication, Inc., 1995), p. 91.
221. Ibid., p. 19.
222. Ibid., p. 3.

223. Ibid., p. 13.
224. Ibid., p. 25.
225. Ibid.
226. Ibid., p. 26.
227. Ibid., p. 35.
228. Allen Johnson, ed. *Dictionary of American Biography* (New York: Charles Scribner's Sons, 1957), Vol. X, p. 506.
229. Quoted in George Grant, *The Patriot's Handbook* (Elkton, MD: Highland Books, 1996), p. 362.
230. Samuel R. Spencer, Jr., *Booker T. Washington and the Negro's Place in American Life* (Boston: Little, Brown and Company, 1955), p. 179.
231. Quoted in Emma Lou Thornbrough, *Booker T. Washington* (New Jersey: Prentice Hall, Inc., 1969), p. 48.
232. Washington in Ibid., p. 16.
233. Ibid., p. 77.
234. Ibid., p. 39.
235. Ibid., p. 80.
236. Quoted in Lewis Copeland, ed., *The World's Great Speeches* (New York: The Book League of America, 1942), p. 332.
237. Washington, Op. Cit., p. 156.
238. Thornbrough, Op. Cit., p. 64.
239. Washington in Ibid., p. 49.
240. Spencer, Op. Cit., p. 51.
241. Ibid., p. 140.
242. Washington, Op. Cit., pp. 53–54.
243. Ibid.
244. Thorngrough, Op. Cit., p. 51.
245. Quoted in Ibid., p. 66.
246. Dewey W. Grantham, ed., *Theodore Roosevelt* (Englewood Cliffs: Prentice Hall Inc., 1971), p. 43
247. George Grant, *Carry a Big Stick: The Uncommon Heroism of Theodore Roosevelt* (Elkton, MD: Highland Books, 1996), p. 99.
248. Ibid., p. 186.
249. Ibid., p. 99.
250. Edward Wagenknecht, *The Seven Worlds of Theodore Roosevelt* (New York: Longmans and Green, 1958), p. 33.
251. Ibid., p. 32.
252. Theodore Roosevelt, *An Autobiography* (New York: Charles Scribner's Sons, 1925), p. 50.
253. Ibid., p. 51.
254. Ibid., p. 54.
255. Grantham, Op. Cit., p. 38.
256. Grant, *Carry a Big Stick,* p. 186.
257. Hermann Hagedorn, *Roosevelt in the Bad Lands* (Boston: Houghton Mifflin Company, 1921), p. 410.
258. Theodore Roosevelt, *Foes of Our Own Household* (New York: Scribners, 1926), p. 152.
259. Roosevelt, *Autobiography,* p. 61.
260. Grant, *Carry a Big Stick,* p. 114.
261. Ibid.
262. G. Wallace Chessman, *Theodore Roosevelt and the Politics of Power* (Boston: Little, Brown and Company, 1969), p. 58.

263. Grantham, Op. Cit., p. 29.
264. Chessman, Op. Cit., pp. 61–62.
265. Grantham, Op. Cit., p. 29.
266. Grant, *Carry a Big Stick,* p. 121.
267. In Nathan Miller, *Theodore Roosevelt: A Life* (New York: William Morris, 1992), p. 142.
268. Ibid., p. 198.
269. Grant, *Carry a Big Stick,* p. 152.
270. Grantham, Op. Cit., p. 10.
271. Roosevelt, *Foes of Our Own Household,* p. 132.
272. Roosevelt in Grant, *Carry,* p. 145.
273. Grantham, Op. Cit., p. 44.
274. Roosevelt, *Autobiography,* p. 55.
275. Grant, *Carry,* p. 64.
276. N. Miller, Op. Cit., pp. 164–165.
277. Ibid., p. 165.
278. Roosevelt, *Autobiography,* pp. 27–28.
279. Ibid.
280. N. Miller, Op. Cit. P. 562.
281. Abraham Kuyper in Frank Vanden Berg, *Abraham Kuyper: A Biography* (Ontario: Paideia Press, 1978), p. 255.
282. Abraham Kuyper, *Christianity: A Total World and Life System* (Marlborough, NH: Plymouth Rock Foundation, 1996), p. 6.
283. Ibid., pp. 11–12.
284. Ibid., p. 14.
285. Ibid., p. 15.
286. Ibid., p. 14.
287. Ibid., p. 18.
288. L. Praamsma, *Let Christ Be King: Reflections on the Life and Times of Abraham Kuyper* (Ontario: Paideia Press, 1978), pp. 153–154.
289. Kuyper, Op. Cit., p. 30.
290. Vanden Berg, Op. Cit., p. 161.
291. Kuyper, Op. Cit. P. 2.
292. Ibid., p. 113.
293. Ibid., pp. 113–114.
294. Ibid., p. 94.
295. Ibid., p. 113.
296. Ibid., p. 114.
297. McKendree R. Langley, *The Practice of Political Spirituality: Episodes from the Public Career of Abraham Kuyper, 1879–1918* (Ontario: Paideia Press, 1984), pp. 26 ff.
298. Ibid., p. 22.
299. Ibid., p. 100.
300. Kuyper, Op. Cit., p. 121.
301. Vanden Berg, Op. Cit., pp. 57–58.
302. Praamsma, Op. Cit., p. 85.
303. Vanden Berg, Op. Cit., pp. 143–144.
304. Praamsma, Op. Cit., p. 65.
305. Vanden Berg, Op. Cit., pp. 17–80.
306. Langley, Op. Cit., pp. 81 ff.
307. Vanden Berg, Op. Cit., p. 230.
308. Ibid., p. 231.

309. Chesterton in Thomas C. Peters, *Battling for the Modern Mind: A Beginner's Chesterton* (St. Louis: Concordia Publishing House, 1994), p. 21.

310. *Credenda Agenda,* Vol. IX, No. 2, p. 3.

311. Masie Ward, *Gilbert Keith Chesterton* (New York: Sheed and Ward, 1943), p. 82.

312. Ibid., ch. 5.

313. Peters, Op. Cit., p. 21.

314. *Credenda Agenda,* Vol. IX, No. 2, p. 2.

315. Alzina Stone Dale, *The Outline of Sanity: A Biography of G.K. Chesterton* (Grand Rapids: William B. Eerdmans Publishing Company, 1982), v.

316. G.K. Chesterton, *The Uses of Diversity: A Book of Essays* (London: Methuen and Company Ltd., 1921), pp. 1 ff.

317. Quoted in Ward, Op. Cit., p. 624.

318. Dale, Op. Cit., p. 224.

319. Ward, Op. Cit., p. 589.

320. Dale, Op. Cit., p. 225.

321. Ibid., p. 226.

322. Chesterton in Ward, Op. Cit., p. 80.

323. Mk. 10: 44.

324. Mt. 18: 4.

325. G.K. Chesterton, *Orthodoxy* (New York: Dodd, Mead and Company, 1940), p. 55.

326. Ibid., p. 23.

327. Peters, Op. Cit., p. 35.

328. Chesterton, *Orthodoxy,* p. 54

329. In Peters, Op. Cit., p. 36.

330. Ibid., p. 161.

331. Ward, Op. Cit., pp. 595–596.

332. Dale, Op. Cit., p. 225.

333. Ibid., p. 226.

334. Chesterton in Ward, Op. Cit., p. 125.

335. Peters, Op. Cit., p. 127.

336. Ibid., p. 128.

337. Ibid.

338. In Ward, Op. Cit., p. 132.

339. In Dale, Op. Cit., p. 70.

340. Peters, Op. Cit., p. 130.

341. Ward, Op. Cit., p. 135.

342. Peters, Op. Cit., p. 129.

343. In Dale, Op. Cit., p. 244.

344. G.K. Chesterton, *Autobiography* (New York: Sheed and Ward, 1936), p. 354.

345. C.S. Lewis, *God In the Dock: Essays on Theology and Ethics* (Grand Rapids: William B. Eerdmans, 1970), p. 200.

346. *Christian History,* Vol. IV, No. 3. P. 6.

347. Terry W. Glaspey, *Not a Tame Lion: The Spiritual Legacy of C.S. Lewis* (Elkton, MD: Highland Books, 1996), p. 233.

348. Ibid., p. 143.

349. George Sayer, *Jack: A Life of C.S. Lewis* (Wheaton, IL: Crossway Books, 1994), pp. 93–94.

350. Roger Lancelyn Green and Walter Hooper, *C.S. Lewis: A Biography* (New York: Harcourt Brace Jovanovich, 1974), pp. 44–45.

351. Lewis, *God In the Dock,* p. 201.

352. Ibid., p. 202.
353. C.S. Lewis, *Mere Christianity* (London: Geoffrey Bles, 1953), p. 121.
354. Glaspey, Op. Cit., pp. 36–37.
355. Ibid.
356. Lewis, *God In the Dock,* pp. 90–91.
357. Ibid., p. 101.
358. C.S. Lewis, *Present Concerns* (San Diego: Harcourt Brace Jovanovich, 1986), p. 65.
359. Ibid., pp. 65–66.
360. See "The Poison of Subjectivism" in C.S. Lewis, *Christian Reflections* (London: Geoffrey Bles, 1967), p. 72.
361. C.S. Lewis, *Miracles: A Preliminary Study* (London: Geoffrey Bles, 1947), p. 27.
362. Ibid., p. 26.
363. Lewis, *Mere Christianity*, p. 42.
364. Lewis in Glaspey, Op. Cit., p. 170.
365. C.S. Lewis, *The Abolition of Man* (London: Geoffrey Bles, 1962), p. 33
366. Lewis, *Christian Reflections,* pp. 74–75.
367. See *Mere Christianity,* ch. 1–2.
368. Ibid., p. 5.
369. Lewis, *Christian Reflections,* p. 77.
370. Lewis, *Mere Christianity,* p. 5.
371. Ibid.
372. Ibid., p. 170.
373. Winston Churchill in Steven F. Hayward, *Churchill On Leadership: Executive Success in the Face of Adversity* (Rocklin, CA: Prima Publishing, 1997), p. 154.
374. In Stephen Mansfield, *Never Give In: The Extraordinary Character of Winston Churchill* (Elkton, MD: Highland Books), p. 75.
375. In Giovanni Costigan, *Makers of Modern England: The Force of Individual Genius in History* (New York: Macmillan Company, 1967), pp. 259–260.
376. Martin Gilbert, ed., *Churchill* (Englewood Cliffs: Prentice-Hall, Inc., 1967), p. 6.
377. Mansfield, Op. Cit., p. 54.
378. Hayward, Op. Cit., p. 30.
379. Mansfield, Op. Cit., p. 57.
380. Ibid., p. 63.
381. Gilbert, Op. Cit., p. 60.
382. Mansfield, Op. Cit., p. 122.
383. Ibid., p. 120.
384. John Pearson, *The Private Lives of Winston Churchill* (New York: Simon and Schuster, 1991), p. 158.
385. Krause, Op. Cit., p. 33.
386. Hayward, Op. Cit., p. 121.
387. Pearson, Op. Cit., p. 81.
388. Mansfield, Op. Cit., p. 43.
389. Ibid., p. 79.
390. Ibid., p. 80.
391. Ibid.
392. Gilbert, Op. Cit., p. 138.
393. Ibid., p. 96.
394. Churchill in Mansfield, Op. Cit., p. 111.
395. Hayward, Op. Cit., p. 9.
396. Ibid.

397. Mansfield, Op. Cit., p. 113.
398. Hayward, Op. Cit., p. 153.
399. Ibid.
400. Mansfield, Op. Cit., p. 111.
401. Ibid., p. 116.
402. Ibid.
403. Hayward, Op. Cit., p. 139.
404. Mansfield, Op. Cit., pp. 162–163.
405. Ibid., p. 170.
406. Ibid.
407. Ibid., p. 164.
408. Seneca in Grant, *The Last Crusader,* p. 47.
409. Cicero, *The Letters and Treatises of Cicero and Pliny* (Vol. IX of Harvard Classics ed., Chicago: P.F. Collier and Son Corporation, 1959), p. 48.
410. Samuel Johnson, *Selected Writings* (New York: Penguin Books, 1968), p. 188.
411. Tacitus, *Annuls,* trans. Alfred John Church and William Jackson Brodribb (Vol. XV of Great Books ed., Chicago: Encyclopedia Britannica, 1952), Bk. III, par. 65.

THOUGHTS ON LEADERSHIP

THOUGHTS ON LEADERSHIP

THOUGHTS ON LEADERSHIP

THOUGHTS ON LEADERSHIP

THOUGHTS ON LEADERSHIP

LEADERSHIP QUALITIES

My Personal Strengths

_____
_____
_____
_____
_____
_____
_____
_____
_____
_____
_____
_____

My Personal Weaknesses

_____
_____
_____
_____
_____
_____
_____
_____
_____
_____

LEADERSHIP JOURNAL

LEADERSHIP JOURNAL

LEADERSHIP JOURNAL

LEADERSHIP JOURNAL

FOR FURTHER STUDY
IN THE
LEADERS IN ACTION SERIES

Never Give In: The Extraordinary Character of Winston Churchill
Stephen Mansfield

Carry a Big Stick: The Uncommon Heroism of Theodore Roosevelt
George Grant

Not a Tame Lion: The Spiritual Legacy of C.S. Lewis
Terry W. Glaspey

Give Me Liberty: The Uncompromising Statesmanship of Patrick Henry
David J. Vaughan

Call of Duty: The Sterling Nobility of Robert E. Lee
J. Steven Wilkins

Then Darkness Fled: The Liberating Wisdom of Booker T. Washington
Stephen Mansfield

For Kirk and Covenant: The Stalwart Courage of John Knox
Douglas Wilson